# The Sweet Teachings of the Blessed Śaṅkarācārya Swami Brahmananda Saraswati

by

LB Shriver

with translation by

Cynthia Ann Humes

*LBS Imprints* *Fairfield, IA*

ISBN: 978-1-304-66200-2



Published in the U.S.A.

Cover art by Roger Humes

LBS Imprints

**LB Shriver**
**(Photo courtesy of Elmker Photo Design)**

## Foreword

LB Shriver was a writer, editor, and publisher right up to the time of his death on May 27, 2013. In the late 1990's, following a banishment and exile by leaders of the Transcendental Meditation movement, LB traveled to India as a journalist-seeker to find answers to questions he had about Swami Brahmananda Saraswati. More commonly known as Guru Dev, Swami Brahmananda Saraswati was the master teacher of Maharishi Mahesh Yogi who served as the Śaṅkarācārya of Jyotir Math of the Himalayas from 1941 to 1953.

While in India, LB sought out some of Guru Dev's still living contemporaries, and in visiting with and directly interviewing those people, LB learned about some transcriptions in Hindi of old wire-recordings of Guru Dev's speeches, as well as some published booklets based on recordings of Guru Dev's public talks. One such example of the latter was a booklet that he found, titled *Śrī Śaṅkarācārya Upadeśāmṛta*, or the *Sweet Teachings of the Blessed Śaṅkarācārya.* Compiled by Rameshwar Prasad Tiwari, *Śrī Śaṅkarācārya Upadeśāmṛta* was published in Allahabad by Dev Bharati Press, and the booklet separated into 108 distinct teachings portions of discourses given by Brahmananda Saraswati during his tenure as *Śaṅkarācārya.*

LB partnered with Professor Cynthia Ann Humes of Claremont McKenna College who translated Tiwari's *Śrī Śaṅkarācārya Upadeśāmṛta* into English and identified the sources of Guru Dev's quotes in the speeches. LB had planned to create a book subsequently that not only featured her translation from Hindi into English, but would include much more, becoming the most complete record and overview of Guru Dev's life and teaching possible. Over many years, LB had spread his burgeoning knowledge of Guru Dev gleaned through his research in many public settings. These materials were intended to eventually become part of an expansive account meant to introduce the life and significance of Guru Dev and the Śaṅkarācārya tradition, Vedanta and its place in Indian philosophy, as well as Guru Dev's legacy within Maharishi Mahesh Yogi's movement. Unfortunately, LB was unable to complete this project before falling gravely ill. When he realized at some point that he was not getting the project done, he decided to help at least make the booklet translation available by sharing with Paul Mason a photocopy of it, and Cynthia Ann Humes shared with Paul Mason her draft translation together with her footnotes identifying many of the Sanskrit sources Guru Dev quoted. Paul Mason proceeded with his own translation, which pleased LB, but LB still hoped some day to bring the more complete book he long envisioned to completion; regrettably, that did not transpire.

Based on discussions I had with LB during his last days, I decided to seek out Professor Humes to construct a form of LB's book that could be offered for publication and accessible for the benefit of all. What follows, then, is first, a lightly edited portion of an introduction written long ago by LB recently discovered among LB's personal effects, and second, the translation by Humes of the "Sweet Teachings of the Blessed *Śaṅkarācārya,*" which is a scholarly work and heavily footnoted. Humes translated the text directly from the photocopy of Tiwari's Hindi booklet, having benefited greatly from discussing with LB about the significance of Guru Dev's teachings based on his original research, as well as reviewing several alternative translations that LB had discovered.

All proceeds from the sale of this bound book are donated as charity to the work in non-profit community service of Sacred Sun Ministries, a 170(b)(1)(a)(vi) charitable organization, of Fairfield, Iowa.

Rest now in Peace, LB Shriver,

*— Doug Hamilton, Fairfield, Iowa — November 2013*

## Introduction

### by LB Shriver

A nearly invisible gap exists in the spiritual and cultural history of the twentieth century a gap which most would never have noticed or felt the need to investigate. Nevertheless, a subtle force has been operating from within that gap, touching the inner life of humanity and shaping its destiny in unanticipated, sometimes surprising ways. That force was embodied in the life of Brahmananda Saraswati.

Despite the fact that the greater portion of his life had been lived in total seclusion, Brahmananda Saraswati (1870-1953) was well known and deeply respected in his own culture. In the last years of his life he served as the Shankaracharya of Jyotir Math in the Himalayas, one of the most highly honored seats of Vedic knowledge. His teaching was profoundly influential throughout India, particularly at the midpoint of the century. A compelling array of facts and arguments makes the case that Brahmananda Saraswati's influence extended far beyond India and persists to this day. Most obvious among these is the fact that he was the spiritual master of Maharishi Mahesh Yogi.

Among the extraordinary images of the sixties, none is more closely associated with the flowering of a new awareness than the smiling faces of Maharishi and the Beatles, pictured at the guru's ashram in fabled Rishikesh. Whether it was a conjunction of celestial influences or an extraordinary stroke of lucky PR, it is hard to imagine how the timing and circumstance of this alliance could have been more favorable for the popularization of meditation around the world.

Celebrity is the lingua franca of the West. To be famous is to be emulated, and the Beatles were as famous as any human being could possibly be so famous that they were even emulated by other celebrities. Transcendental

Meditation, the simple technique into which Maharishi initiated his followers spread like wildfire through Western popular culture. The roster of smiling famous faces grew to include the Beach Boys, Donovan, The Rolling Stones, Bob Dylan, The Doors, Mia Farrow, Peter Fonda, Clint Eastwood, Peggy Lee, Mary Tyler Moore, Merv Griffin, Joe Namath, Arthur Ashe, and Hell's Angels founding president Sonny Barger.

Meditation, which had previously been of interest only to the esoteric fringe, became accepted into the mainstream of Western thought and practice. Transcendental Meditation affiliated programs penetrated virtually every level of society, from the classrooms at Stanford to the cell blocks of Folsom Prison and the board rooms at General Motors.

Controversial almost from the beginning, Maharishi has been described both as a fraud and as the greatest saint to walk the earth in ten thousand years and everything in between. By nearly every measure he was the most prominent, and in that sense, most important guru to bring Eastern wisdom to the West. He has been universally acknowledged as a popularizer, but is less commonly appreciated for the extent to which he has disseminated the traditional Vedic knowledge of India.

An important component of the teaching conventions employed by Maharishi has been the puja, or ceremony of gratitude to the tradition of masters represented by Brahmananda Saraswati. Performed in Sanskrit in front of a picture of Maharishi's master, the ceremony confers upon him the status of guru for the initiate. In other words, Brahmananda Saraswati, not Maharishi Mahesh Yogi, is given credit for the transmission of knowledge, and he is therefore referred to by Maharishi and his initiates as Guru Dev, the customary honorific for one's personal master.

Although public interest in Transcendental Mediation peaked in the early 1970s, it continued to draw a steady stream of celebrities, reaching as far backward into the collective imagination as silent film star Greta Garbo, and as far forward toward contemporary times as the comic genius Andy Kaufman, master magician Doug Henning, shock-radio host Howard Stern, rock musician Lenny Kravitz, film director David Lynch, and pop diva Madonna. In the United States, more than two million have learned the practice of Transcendental Meditation; worldwide, five million. And all were instructed at the lotus feet of Swami Brahmananda Saraswati.

The purpose of this book is to shed some light on the life and teachings of one of the great masters of the Vedic tradition of India. It will succeed only to the extent that the reader sees Brahmananda Ji's life in the context of the tradition he represented a tradition which is ancient with respect to its wellsprings and completely contemporary with respect to its impact on world consciousness.

Books about gurus have become commonplace in Western culture, and they are written from wildly diverging points of view: the devotee seeks to glorify, the critic aims to discredit, and the historian endeavors to illuminate. Each of these approaches may be in evidence here but the intention is to favor the historical.

Good history thrives on first-hand accounts, source documents, and the passage of time for historical perspective. This effort makes use of all of three in the attempt to achieve a kind of wholeness in the treatment of its subject matter, but does not pretend to achieve completeness. In particular, we do not have access to the private teachings that passed between the master and his closest disciples. Nevertheless the talks which Brahmananda Saraswati gave during the course of his public career provide clear and detailed insights into the nature of his thinking and the tradition which shaped it. These public talks form the core of this book; the introductory and supporting material are offered to help understand the cultural and philosophical matrix from which they were delivered.

As for the biographical portion of our narrative: the intention here is only to create an outline of the main events of Brahmananda Saraswati's life so that the readeræs intuition can fill in the gaps. Naturally, some difficult choices have been made about which events should be included, which stories should be told. This is not, after all, the story of a young boy running off to join the circus. Rather it is the story of one who set off before the age of nine to realize the Supreme according to tradition, a journey to the land from which no traveler ever returns.

Stories of saints and yogis are traditionally replete with miracles, apparitions, supernormal abilities, and encounters with the Divine. Brahmananda Ji's story follows this time-honored pattern. For the sake of brevity, we have chosen not to include all the available anecdotes relating to Brahmananda Ji's life as a young sadhu, and will focus instead on those which give the clearest insights into the dominant themes of his life particularly the themes of self-sufficiency and support of Nature. Some of the more exotic stories have been left out because, though fascinating, they are more or less incidental to the main narrative. However, even such stories as those which we have included may depart so radically from the layman's daily experience that they are assumed to be apocryphal, allegorical, or just plain fabricated. How are they to be regarded?

The principle source for this narration is *The Whole Thing, The Real Thing*, a short biography by Rameswar Tiwari, who also compiled the talks contained in this volume. Tiwari's biography is apparently drawn from the same material as this collection: i.e., the talks given by Brahmananda Ji to his disciples, and written down as he spoke. Therefore we feel that it can be regarded substantially as his own account, and we present it on its own terms.

Another valuable source is *Strange Facts About a Great Saint*, by Dr. Raj R. P. Varma, who was also a direct disciple of Brahmananda Saraswati and the uncle of Maharishi Mahesh Yogi. Essentially the same as Tiwari's account,

Varma Ji's rendering includes some details unavailable in Tiwari's, although the English is somewhat more labored.

Simply put, we believe this story to be authentic. Its meaning and interpretation, however, remain the responsibility of the reader.

Brahmananda Saraswati: A Brief Biography

Like Siddhartha, the Buddha, who lived in the sixth century BCE, Brahmananda Saraswati seemed destined to wealth and privilege. Born on Thursday, 21 December 1870, young Rajaram was the treasured child of the Mishra family, prominent Brahmins who lived in the North Indian village of Gana, located near Ayodhya, the birthplace of Lord Rama.

Also like the Buddha, young Rajaram's precocious philosophical nature set him on a path far removed from that envisioned by his parents. A somber and reflective youth, he received a severe emotional jolt at the death of his beloved grandfather, who died when Rajaram was seven. Even though his parents tried to shield him from viewing his grandfather's lifeless corpse, the young by was led be a sympathetic servant  to a window from which he could see the shrouded body being carried away, accompanied by the chant, Ram, Naam, Satya hai Lord, Thy name is Truth.

The young boy tried to penetrate the meaning of these mysteries death, God, truth and became convinced that the life to which he had been born was shallow and ephemeral. At age eight he underwent the traditional Upanayana ceremony in which he became twice born and received the sacred thread, which marked his eligibility for higher religious learning. Then he was sent to Varanasi (Benares) to undertake his study of the Vedas. The atmosphere of that holy city only confirmed for him that his vocation was spiritual, not worldly, but not long after he arrived there he was shocked to learn that his familyÆs plans for his future now included an arranged marriage.

The truth of Rajaram's life was stark: he had come into this world with an exceptional degree of spiritual wakefulness, and he was never, in practical terms, a serious candidate for a normal life. He understood this long before his parents did, and when faced with the impending reality of a life he could not live, he set off for the Himalayas.

Traveling alone, unencumbered with material resources of any kind, Rajaram made his way West and Northward along the banks of the Ganga. It was an arduous journey by any standard. When Bhagirathi, the River Goddess, suggested that he stop and refresh himself with her waters, [he replied, Mother, it is with your grace alone that I can make this long journey. Let me not get into the habit of stopping. Let me reach soon a cave in the Himalayas where I can sit and find my life's fulfillment.] He bowed in reverence and moved on.

Taking only occasional sips of Ganga water to sustain himself, he arrived after about three days at a small village, where he caught the attention of the local zaminder, who asked him, [Who are you?]

[Why do you want to know? What is your intention?

All I want to know is who you are and why are you going in such a great hurry on this rugged path at such an odd time.

The young ascetic said, You are not in a position to know whether this is the right path or the wrong path, the right time or the wrong time. "Sufficient for you to know that I am traveling from Kashi [Varanasi] to the Himalayas to meditate. Go and mind your own business and don't trouble me for nothing."

The zamindar, taken aback somewhat, mustered courage enough to say softly, Maharaj, may I ask you when and where on the way you have begged for food?

He got the reply, So far the Ganga water has been food and my drink.

Then come and have some food and rest before you go further. That will give me satisfaction. Moreover, it's going to be dark.

I'm not going to knock at anyone's door for food. As for satisfaction, I cannot believe that your giving me a meal would give you satisfaction. Satisfaction means that no desires remain and after that no desires arise. Your giving me alms is not going to give you satisfaction. That can only come if you know the Supreme Essence, knowing which all else is known, and obtaining which nothing remains unattainable. So make such efforts that bring you real satisfaction.]

The older man arranged for some milk to be brought, and Rajaram offered two-thirds to Bhagarithi in return for the water he had drunk on the first three days of his journey. This so moved the River Goddess that she granted him a boon that he would never have to subsist on just water again.

After three days of travel, Rajaram arrived at Prayag [Allahabad] and the confluence of the sacred rivers. He had not gone unnoticed in his travels: though still a child, he had and air of maturity and spiritual purpose which others could not fail to notice. In addition, his family deeply worried over his sudden departure had circulated his description to police stations throughout the area and offered a reward for his return. A policeman from Allahabad attempted to take him into custody and return him for the reward, but Rajaram confounded him with the intensity of his purpose and the profundity of the logic with which he defended himself. Humbled, the officer put the boy on the train for Haridwar. Soon after he arrived there, Rajaram was accosted by yet another policeman. As before, the officer was no match for the pilgrim. The next day, however, Rajaram was apprehended on his way to Rikikesh. This time greed won out, and the runaway was sent home to his family.

Rajaram's parents were overjoyed at his return, only to be dismayed at his insistence that he be allowed to continue his spiritual quest. Unable to convince him otherwise, they called in the family priest to reason with the youth. Panditji lost the argument, however, and in the process became convinced not only that the boy was a spiritual prodigy, but that to impede his pilgrimage would be a mistake. Eventually the family was won over as well. Rajaram's mother admonished only that, should he change his mind and decide to take up the life of the householder, he could simply come home right away and that he not beg for alms. Two days later, he was gone.

After a few days at Prayag, he moved on to the Haridwar, and then to Rikikesh, Gateway to the Himalayas. There he decided to pause and see if he could find a suitable guru. The traditional criteria of appropriateness in a teacher are knowledge of the Vedic texts and a high degree of personal realization, i.e., direct experience of the Divine. Rajaram had two criteria of his own, as well: his teacher should be a life celibate and one who was free of anger.

Rikikesh was home to many famous gurus and spiritual aspirants of all persuasions. Rajaram made the rounds to visit them all, but found none quite to his liking. In one incident well known to devotees of Brahmananda Saraswati, the boy visited a famous Dandi Swami, a renunciate whose vows included the foresaking the use of fire. After greeting the yogi respectfully, the young pilgrim asked if he could please have some fire. The Swami replied angrily: any fool should know that Dandi Sannyasis don't keep fire. The youth calmly inquired where all the heat was coming from if no fire was being kept there.

Once again the adult had been humbled before the child. The Swami immediately understood both the nature of his error and the brilliance of the aspirant he knew that the best of gurus would be lucky to have such a disciple, even once in a lifetime. Swamiji asked the young boy to stay, and for several days gave him instruction in yoga. They got along well, but nevertheless, the swami had failed the test for anger, and the boy knew that he must not compromise his high standards.

The quest continued, ranging far and wide. Eventually it took the pilgrim further north to Uttarkashi, where he finally found his ideal in the form of Swami Krishnanand, a Dandi Sannyasi from Sringeri Math. The youth surrendered to his master and received initiation from him.

This marks the end of the story of Rajaram and begins the story of Brahma Chaitanya Brahmachari.

The traditional relationship between sishya (disciple) and acharya (master) has few parallels in the modern societies of the West. The master is not merely a teacher, but assumes a parental role as well. The disciple lives with the master and other disciples in the master's ashram, and success in the enterprise they undertake together depends not only on the knowledge, skill, and good intentions of the master, but on the love, faith, and surrender of the disciple as well.

Brahma Chaitanya Brahmachari, known less formally as Maharaj Shri, was exceptionally devoted to his master, and the bond that developed between the two was extraordinary. Maharaj Shri displayed a rare capacity to intuit the needs of his master and act accordingly, and thus endeared himself to the Guruji to the highest degree. In fact, the very closeness of their relationship created potential problems in the ashram, because of the possibility that some of the older disciples might become jealous.

Guruji recognized that his young brahmachari was ready for advanced instruction, and staged a minor incident in the ashram as a pretext for sending Maharaj Shri to a cave three miles away so he could pursue his new program undisturbed. The other disciples assumed that Maharaj Shri had been banished for bad behavior, and were later chagrined to discover that the depth of his devotion had won him favored standing with their master.

By the age of twenty-five the brahmachari had completed his study of the scriptures and had discovered the truth about his innermost Self. Maharaj Shri and his master left Uttarkashi and traveled about in the vicinity of Rikikesh. Tiwari's biography contains several brief anecdotes from this period, in which the young sadhu was apparently learning the role of the holy man in the world at large.

In one of the more amusing stories, Maharaj Shri was sitting in meditation on a wintry day in Rikikesh when a wealthy businessman draped a shawl around his shoulders. The sadhu opened his eyes and asked what the shawl was all about; the businessman said he was acting on the axiom that a rupee given in charity to a mahatma returns to the donor thousandfold. By giving this one shawl he hoped to get a thousand in return. Maharaj Shri handed him back the shawl, remarking drily that this was the first and he would see what he could to about the remaining 999.

At the age of thirty-six Brahma Chaitanya Brahmachari was formally initiated into the monastic order by his master, taking his vows at the Kumbh Mela at Prayag (circa 1906). From this time on he was known as Shri Swami Brahmanand Saraswati Maharaj Swami Brahmananda Saraswati.

Even though he had been living almost exclusively as a total recluse, Brahmananda Ji's presence was beginning to be felt among the people. Wherever he went, they wanted his darshan and his blessings. Still, he continued his pattern of reclusiveness. Among the many who came to see him, often the only ones who succeeded were those who sat and waited patiently long after the others had given up.

On reading Tiwari's biography of Brahmananda Saraswati, one naturally wonders if the devotee's enthusiasm has perhaps inflated the legend of his master. In this regard, it is fascinating to read an account by an objective and completely authoritative observer, as found *in Living With the Himalayan Masters*, by Swami Rama. [The Himalayan Institute Press; Honesdale, PA;@1978, 1999, Himalayan International Institute of Yoga Science and Philosophy].

The Wave of Bliss

I once visited Chitrakoot, one of the holy places there, according to the epic Ramayana, Lord Rama live during his exile. This place is situated on the Vindhya Range, one of the longest mountain ranges in India. According to ancient tradition, Vairagi sadhus visit Brindaban and Chitrakoot. Brindabam for those who live Krishna and Chitrakoot for those who love Rama. In another part of the Vindhya Range, in a holy place called Vinhyachal, there lived many Shakti worshipers. Traveling toward the forests of the Reva State, I went to the Satana forest and there met a swami who was very handsome and highly educated in the Vedantic and yogic tradition. He knew the scriptures and was a very brilliant sadhaka (spiritual practitioner). He was later nominated as Shankaracharya of Jyotirmayapitham, which is in the Himalayas on the way to Badrinath. His name was Bramananda Saraswati.

He used to live only on germinated gram seeds mixed with a little bit of salt. He lived on a hillock in a small natural cave near a mountain pool. I was led by the villagers to that place, but I did not find anyone there and became disappointed. The next day I went again and found a few footprints on the edge of the pool made by his wooden sandals. I tried, but I could not track the footprints. Finally on the fifth day of the effort early in the morning before sunrise, I went back to the pool and found him taking a bath. I greeted him by saying, Namo narayan, which is a commonly used salutation among swamis meaning, I bow to the divinity in you. He was observing silence so he motioned for me to follow him to his small cave and I did so gladly. This was the eighth day of his silence, and after staying the night with him, he broke his silence and I gently spoke to him about the purpose of my visit. I wanted to know how he was living and the ways and methods of his spiritual practices. During our conversation, he started talking to me about Sri Vidya, the highest of paths followed only by accomplished Sanskrit scholars of India. It is a path which joins Raja yoga, Kundalini yoga, Bhakti yoga and Advaita Vedanta. There are two books recommended by the teachers of this path, *The Wave of Bliss and the Wave of Beauty*; the compilation of the two books is called *Saundarya Lahari* in Sanskrit. There is another part of this literature called *Prayoga Shastra*, (The book of yogic practices and application.) which is in manuscript form and found only in the Mysore and Baroda libraries. No scholar can understand these spiritual yogic poems without the help of a competent teacher who himself practices these teachings.

Later on, I found that Sri Vidya and Madhuvidya are spiritual practices know to a very few only ten to twelve people in all India.

Swami Rama had traveled throughout India as a young sadhu and personally met with the top holy men of his time. He himself became the Shankaracharya of Karvirpitham in South India in 1949, but left that position after two years because the pressures of the public duties were stifling to him. He later established his ashram in Ram Nagar, just downstream and on the opposite bank from Shankaracharya Nagar, Maharishi's ashram in Rishikesh.

The years passed, and the atmosphere of sanctity and wisdom surrounding Brahmananda Ji continued to deepen. His own master, Swami Krishnanand Saraswati, now treated him as an equal. His Guruji also encouraged him to come out of his seclusion from time to time.

You have spent enough of your lifetime in forests and mountains. Now spend more of your time in towns and cities so that people can derive the benefit of your vast learning. As it is, you are unmatched in answering questions and clearing the doubts of the people.

As the public career of Brahmananda Saraswati continued to unfold, the central aspects of his character likewise became more apparent. Prominent among these was his self-sufficiency. As he had promised his mother, he had never stretched his hand before any man to ask for charity, and as the River Goddess had promised him, he had never been without sustenance even in the depths of the forest. Eyewitness accounts from disciples who had traveled with him, far from the amenities of civilization, said that a pot of cream or a basket of fruit would mysteriously appear when needed, but the gifts could never be traced to a donor in the villages from which they presumably had come.

When presiding over his ashram, Brahmandaji made it an inviolable rule that no gifts of money would be accepted from those who came for puja, and posted a sign to that effect. Instead, he invited those who came to him for blessings or advice to offer him their sins. After all, he said, people value their sins above all else, as can be seen by how reluctant they are to part with them. Give me your sins, he said, and I will give you the path to liberation.

Even when approached with the necessity of financing the administrative needs of the ashram, he refused to resort to fundraising yet the funds were always there when needed. This phenomenon hardly went unnoticed, and people began to speculate the Brahmananda Ji had a special siddhi for wealth. A rumor took shape that he had a magic box that was filled with rupees whenever he opened it.

Box or no box, Maharaj Shri made it clear to all that he depended only on God for his needs. When God gives, he gives all that is required: the whole thing the real thing.

Brahmananda Ji's self-sufficiency was not just in material things. He lacked nothing, wanted nothing from any person, and owed nobody any favors. His interest in fame and fortune were nil. Perhaps it was this very indifference to the world which qualified him so richly for the role he was to play as the Shankaracharya of Jyotir Math. In any event, a lifetime of austerity and asceticism had cultured a personality of formidable spiritual resources, and these were the treasures that Brahmananda Saraswati brought to the throne of Shankaracharya.

The Vedic Tradition

At the beginning of our introduction we said that Brahmananda Saraswati embodied a subtle force which had been influencing human destiny throughout the twentieth century, specifically, that force is the Vedic tradition of India, of which the Shankaracharya tradition is a central element. To understand the significance of Brahmananda Ji's life and training, one must have some idea of what the Vedic tradition is and why we regard Brahmananda Saraswati as its representative.

Despite centuries of exploration and imperialism by the West, and despite the impact of modernization and global communications, East and West remain separated by their views of Indian history. These disputes are not limited to point of view, but include disagreements about basic chronology and the factuality of major historical events.

Although the extreme sanctity accorded to the Vedas by Hindus has been duly noted by Western scholars, the texts themselves have generally been regarded as impenetrable. Among others taking exception to this view, Sri Aurobindo Ghose (1872-1950) wrote eloquently on this problem in the *Secret of the Veda* (Sri Aurobundo Ashram, Pondicherry, 1971, p 2):

In the course of several thousands of years there have been at least three considerable attempts, entirely differing from each other in their methods and results, to fix the sense of these ancient litanies. One of these is prehistoric in time and exists only by fragments in the in the Brahmanas and Upanishads; but we possess in its entirety the traditional interpretation of the Indian scholar Sayana and we have in our own day the interpretation constructed after an immense labour and conjecture by modern European scholarship. Both of them present one characteristic in common, the extraordinary incoherence and poverty of sense which their results stamp on the ancient hymns. When we come to the hymns as a whole we seem to be in the presence of men who, unlike the early writers of other races, were incapable of coherent and natural expression or of connected thought.

Yet these obscure and barbarous compositions have had the most splendid good fortune in all of literary history. They have been the reputed source not only of some of the worldÆs richest and most profound religions, but of some of its subtlest metaphysical philosophies. In the fixed tradition of thousands of years they have been revered as the origin and standard of all that can be held as authoritative and true in Brahmana and Upanishad, in Tantra and Purana, in the doctrines of great philosophical schools and in the teachings of famous saints and sages. The name borne by them was Veda, the knowledge, the received name for the highest spiritual truth of which the human mind is capable.

It is interesting to contrast Aurobindo's view with that of a modern secular thinker, Jawarlal Nehru. Written by Pandit Nehru in1944, while he was being held as a political prisoner in the Ahmadnagar Fort prison, *The Discovery of India* includes his musings on the nature of the Vedas:

> The RigVeda, the first of the Vedas, is probably the earliest book that humanity possesses. In it we can find the first outpourings of the human mind, the glow of poetry, the rapture at natureÆs loveliness and mystery.
>
> Yet behind the Rig Veda itself lay ages of civilized existence and thought, during which the Indus Valley and the Mesopotamian and other civilizations had grown. It is appropriate, therefore, that there should be this dedication in the Rig Veda: To the seers, our ancestors, the first path-finders!
>
> These Vedic hymns have been described by Rabindranath Tagore as a poetic testament of a people's collective reaction to the wonder and awe of existence. A people of vigorous and unsophisticated imagination awakened at the very dawn of civilization to a sense of the inexhaustible mystery that is implicit in life.

Still another approach to the Veda emphasizes *uncreated*, or revealed, status. According to this line of thinking, the verses of the Veda were not *composed* by poets, but were *cognized* by the Vedic seers. They are nothing less than the immutable laws of nature, transmitted from generation to generation through the oral tradition.

Although the ôrevealedö status of the Vedic literature sets it apart from the objective traditions prominent in the West, commonalities exist between them. Even in the Western intellectual tradition, the laws of nature are acknowledged to be in the transcendent realm. That is to say, they are to be inferred or calculated within the consciousness of the scientist, but can never be located as objects within material creation. We see the effects of a law of nature, but we never see the law itself. Since the laws of nature exist in the transcendental realm, as pure impulses of energy and intelligence, they are beyond the reach of microscopes, telescopes, and all varieties of scientific instrumentation.

The one instrument capable of detecting these impulses is the human nervous systemùbut only after it has been disciplined and cultured according to the rigorous precepts of Vedic teachings. Such a nervous system is capable of detecting that which lies beyond the reach of the senses. Tradition says that the *richa-s* of the Veda appear spontaneously in the awareness of the seer who is worthy of them, and that the seer is then inspired to vocalize his experience. Thus, Vedic chanting is regarded as an effect of
Vedic cognition, just as an apple's fall is regarded as an effect of gravity. These vocalizations, or chanting, are said to accurately correspond to the mathematical qualities of the laws of nature that inspire them. That is, the frequency of the sounds, the rhythm of the meter and all facets of the rishiÆs performance are determined by the specific qualities of the natural law which generate them.

Among the implications of this view is the idea that Vedic cognition represents a path of knowledge complementary to the Western scientific method, but free of many of its limitations. Those among the readers of this account who were introduced to the Vedic tradition through Transcendental Meditation will recognize this view as that which is taught by Maharishi Mahesh Yogi, whose teachings will be discussed later in this introduction.

Many historical factors could have contributed to the undervaluing of the Vedas in the West. Among them, the moral perspectives of imperialism and racism that were part of the legacy of India's conquerors over the centuries, the last but not least of which was the British Empire.

European imperialism moved forward under the unquestioned assumptions that ancient Greece was the pinnacle of human civilization and that the world would indeed by a better place if the uncivilized heathen could be recast in the mold of European culture. This is not to say that India did not benefit in any way from, for example, Western education, but the efforts of Lord Macaulay in the 1800s to introduce Western education at the expense of Indian traditional education had a devastating effect on Indian culture. Neither does one have to be a hardened cynic to see that the moral faṛade of imperialism in every generation was a convenient cover for the wholesale theft of the wealth that rightfully belonged to the Indian people. Tremendous fortunes were made during the imperial period, but rarely by Indians. Had this treasure not lay in wait of imperial pillagers, it is doubtful that the moral imperatives of educating and converting the aboriginals would have been carried out with such enthusiasm and devotion.

In short, according to *The Wealth and Poverty of Nations: Why Some Are So Rich and Some So Poor* (W W Norton & Company; New York, London: 1998), the historical and cultural biases of the West was such that even though much of the most important work on Indian history, "has been done by Indian scholars, yet these, ironically, have had to rely almost exclusively on European records and accounts. Almost no written documentation comes to us from the Indian side."

In recent years, anticolonialist critics have made much of the alleged misdeeds of Western curiosity, putting scholars, spies and diplomatic agents in the same knave's basket. Insofar as this critique holds that only insiders can know the truth about their societies, it is wrong. Insofar as one uses this claim to discredit the work of intellectual adversaries, it is polemical and antiscientific. But insofar as it points to the instrumental value and power on information for good and for bad, it makes an important point. If these scholars could not make sense of something in the *Vedas* they usually blamed the Vedic seers for being unintelligible, not themselves for missing something of the right way of approach to such mystical teachings. The dissected the *Vedas* according to a materialistic and intellectual mind, not by a mind sensitive to the spiritual life or to symbolic language. Hence we can still say that the real meaning of the *Vedas* is as yet unknown to us. Such translators and interpreters mainly served to categorize Vedic grammar but they did not have the background to understand the spiritual secrets of the *Vedas.*

## Shankara and the Shankaracharya Tradition

The Vedic Tradition is regarded as unique not only for the antiquity of its roots but also for the fact that it is a living tradition with continuous, unbroken links to the past. It has been transmitted across the centuries through the teachings of an illustrious lineage of masters, none of whom is more generally revered than Adi Shankara, the first among many to carry his name.

Where Shankara is concerned, it is somewhat difficult to distinguish the historical from the mythical. It is generally agreed that he was born in Kerala, Southwest India. He is said to have lived only 32 years, but by the age of 16 he had completed commentaries on the Upanishads, the Brahma Sutras, and the Bhagavad Gita—three of the most important scriptures of Hinduism.

The chronology of the life of Adi Shankara and the timeline of succession in the tradition of teachers which he established marks another major point of disagreement between the East and West. Western scholars typically ascribe to Shankara a birthdate of 788 CE. According to Indian tradition, however, Shankara was a contemporary of Lord Buddha, approximately 2,500 years ago.

*Our Spiritual Heritage* by Lynn D. Napper is a recounting of the Shankaracharya Tradition from the birth of Adi Shankara (the first) through modern times. Napper makes note of the discrepancy between Eastern and Western accounts of Shankara's life and teaching by taking recourse to the records found within the monastic orders:

> According to records of the succession of Sankaracharyas kept in Kanchi Math, Kalika Math, and at Jagannath Puri, Sankara was born in 509 B.C. This is corroborated in all three centers. Who would be more interested in the time of Sankara than those very centers he set up to propagate his teachings? Also, the record of the genealogy of the Kings of Tibet mention a visit by Sankara in the 6th century B.C.
>
> The records kept at Sarada Math in Sringeri indicate that Sankara was born about one thousand nine hundred years ago, but there are several discrepancies in their records rendering them an unreliable source of information
>
> One of the difficulties historians and scholars have in tracing the history of Sankara is the fact that he set up a monastic system of succession in four corners of India to perpetuate the wisdom. The word acharya means teacher. The heads of these four centers or Maths are called Sankaracharya, a title meaning the teachers of Sankara's wisdom. Sankara himself is commonly known as Sankaracharya, because he was the first. Sometimes he is called Adi Sankaracharya meaning "the first Sankara teacher."
>
> Historians find it difficult to believe that anyone who only lived 32 years could have produced so many commentaries and writings. Sankara is said to b the author of over one hundred fifty books. They donÆt take into consideration that he was an avatar of Siva, so what could be impossible for him? He could even refer in his writing to events that had not yet occurred! It is possible, however, that some of the

writing attributed to him may actually be the work of a later Sankaracharya.

There was a very prolific Sankaracharya named Abhinava who lived from 788 to 840 A.D. It is quite likely that the historians and scholars base their arguments on the date of Sankara's birth on the confusion between Adi Sankara and Abhinava Sankaracharya because it is generally agreed among scholars and historians that Sankara was born in 788 A.D. Abhinava was the 33rd successor in his math after Sankaracharya.

The date of Sankaracharya's birth that is accepted by members of the order is 509 B.C. He passed from this earth at the age of 32, in the year 477 B.C. Before doing so, he set up his four major disciples as heads of centers of learning in the four corners of India, according to Siva's instructions to him.

Adi Shankara was not a religious hermit and scholar, but an active and peripatetic teacher who advanced his philosophy by debating the great scholars and teachers of his time and winning. One story of his prowess reveals something of the status he was accorded by his peers.

Shankara paid a visit to Sharada Nilaya in Kashmir known as Sarvajna Peetha (the seat of the all knowing). Those who are not all-knowing are not entitled to sit on it; no one could claim to be an expert in any religion or philosophy without sitting on it. Shankara did not wish to show himself off as Sarvajna. He felt that Shri Sharada Nilaya with Sarvajna Peetha was by itself a place worthy of visit by all devotees. Besides, Kashmir is the crown of Bharat. So he resolved to go there, lest the ancient Hindu religion should perish there.

There are four gates in four directions for entering Sharada Nilaya. Eminent scholars and philosophers had entered it from various directions and had established their scholarly merit. But no one so far had adorned the chair of Sarvajna. And also until then no one had even attempted to enter the temple through the Southern gate. Maybe this gate was waiting for Acharya Shankara who was from the south! Scholars of many groups and communities were waiting for him in the premises of Shri Sharada Nilaya. All were filled with a feeling of reverence to see him who was learned in both Jnana and Vijnana. Yet the scholars in religious philosophies of Jaina, Bouddha, Samkya, Yoga, Nyaya and Vaisheshika confronted him at the time of his entry to the temple. Shankara defeated them all in philosophical debate and then entered the temple through the Southern gate.

**LB Shriver's Initial Short Written Introduction to *The Brahmananda Saraswati Discourses:***

This collection necessarily reflects only faintly what must surely have been one of the most unique and powerful personalities of the 20th Century. Transcribed by hand by his disciples as he spoke and translated nearly half a century later, the gap is bridged as much by intuition as by grammar and linguistic conventions. The 108 discourses do not comprise flawlessly articulated *shastra* nor a meticulously crafted philosophical treatise, but are instead the legacy of a teacher who spoke simply and directly to the people. Despite the inevitable redundancies common to compilations of this kind, and despite the problems inherent in translating between two highly dissimilar languages, we believe nevertheless that something will be communicated from heart to heart.

— *LB Shriver*

# The Sweet Teachings of the Blessed Śaṅkarācārya Swami Brahmananda Saraswati

## *Teaching #1*

### Only he who is happy can make another happy

The individual soul[1] can be genuinely happy only through connection with Paramātmā,[2] because in Paramātmā lies the culmination of happiness

ॐ

One can only share what one possesses. Begging for money from a poor man is folly. Just as one can obtain wealth only from the wealthy, wisdom (*vidyā*) can only be gained from the wise. Happiness,[3] too, can only be gained from that great storehouse of happiness, who is none other than Bhagavān.[4]

---

[1]I translate *jīva* as the "individual soul," following common non-dual philosophical (*Advaita Vedānta*) explanations. Under the influence of ignorance or *avidyā*, *ātman* appears as *jīva*, the individual soul subject to transmigration.

[2] I have left the term *Paramātma* (literally, "great self" or "great soul") untranslated and unitalicized throughout the text to serve as a proper noun so that the reader may interpret Guru Dev's meaning independently.

[3] The adjective Guru Dev employs here is *sukhī*, a Hindi loan word from the Sanskrit, *sukha*, which may be inflected as both adjective and noun. *Sukha* is a natural pair to the Sanskrit *duḥkha*, appearing in Hindi as the simplified pronunciation, *dukha*. *Sukha* means having a good wheel axel, or comfortable; the second *duḥkha* means having a bad wheel axel, or fraught with hardship. In philosophical discourse, the original Sanskrit *duḥkha* connotes existential hardship, suffering, discomfort, and dissatisfaction, referencing the experience of a chariot rider, who when one wheel is bad, experiences the journey as lurching and uncomfortable; *sukha* refers to the experience of a smooth ride. This pair is

Within *saṃsāra*,[5] no one can be happy who is not a devotee favored with the grace of Bhagavān.[6] Only devotees of dear, spiritual Paramātmā experience this happiness; all others are ensnared with some type of dissatisfaction. In *saṃsāra*, no truly happy person can be found. The person who lacks something considers another who has what he lacks to be happy. Yet one sees that that other person does not actually consider himself to be happy. Whoever is childless assumes those with children are happy, yet just ask the person with a child how happy he is with his children. It is well known that in reality, there is no happiness in worldly objects. The true form[7] of happiness is that which has the true form of Being, Consciousness, and Bliss (*sat chit ānanda*),[8] Paramātmā, and only by coming into connection with Paramātmā can the individual soul (*jīva*) be happy; there is no other path to being happy. This Paramātmā is like a general merchant[9] who can deliver any object desired without ever running out of

---

also commonly found in Buddhist texts composed in the language of Pali, which has a slightly different spelling from both Sanskrit and Hindi. I reserve the English term "bliss" for *ānanda*.

[4] *Bhagavān* is often translated "Blessed Lord." I have left this term untranslated and unitalicized to serve as a proper noun throughout the text so that the reader may interpret Guru Dev's meaning independently.

[5] The term *saṃsāra* is sometimes glossed "the world." Yet its meaning implies not just birth in this world, but as its Sanskrit root of "streaming" connotes, *saṃsāra* is the flow of continuous rebirths the individual soul experiences as well. I have thus consistently retained the term *saṃsāra* so the reader is free to interpret it contextually.

[6] I translate *kṛpā* here as "favor" or "grace." It can also connote "kindness."

[7] I have glossed *svarūpa* as "true form," and *svabhāva* as "self-nature," or in certain contexts, "own nature."

[8]This famous triad is invoked continuously in the *Advaita Vedānta* tradition, and is found in the original text in parentheses.

[9] Guru Dev used the English term "general merchant" in the original.

supplies. But to obtain his blessing (*kṛpā*), we must strive methodically,[10] for nothing can result from merely reciting the glorifications[11] of Paramātmā alone. Can anyone become rich [simply] by continuously chanting an invoice?

To expect to gain happiness from worldly-minded persons is a mistake. How can he who is himself unhappy make others happy? The happiness which appears in *saṃsāra* is relative.[12] One person is happy in one aspect, whereas someone else is [happy] in another.

If one must beg for happiness from someone, then only beg from a source that can give all happiness. Remember that whoever is inclined towards Paramātmā can obtain happiness and peace in *saṃsāra*; no one else. Searching for happiness in *saṃsāra* is like trying to quench your thirst by collecting drops of dew.

---

[10]The term modifying effort or *prayatna* is *vidhivat*, referring to due lawful behavior; here, the religious rules.

[11] The term *māhātmya* denotes a specific genre of Hindu devotional praise stories, commonly translated "glorifications."

[12] In the Sanskrit, *sāpekṣa* means "dependent," or "relative."

# *Teaching #2*

**Having entered *saüsàra*, now listen up and use all your skill so that you won't have to re-enter these pots of excrement and urine**[13]

Only by the favor of Bhagavān can one be released from the porter's lot.[14]

ॐ

Through how many lives have we carried the heavy load of rebirth ... at times in the body of an elephant weighing five tons, at other times in the body of an ant weighing a scant half gram, still other times in the body of a human being, or at other times in some other body ... Whatever load onc may bc carrying can be removed only by the blessing (*kṛpā*) of Bhagavān.

Conduct yourself such that in this very lifetime you may obtain the blessing of Bhagavān, and are not forced to incarnate again in a body of urine and excrement. This will happen only if you follow Bhagavān's commandments. The teaching of the *Vedaśāstra* is verily the command of Bhagavān.

Keep to your own *dharma* in accordance with your *varṇa* and stage of life,[15] and at all times remember Bhagavān.[16]

---

[13] Many sages from Indic traditions that stress freedom from the cycle of rebirth refer to the body as a "pot of excrement and urine" to shock their listener from complacency and unexamined attachment to human birth. See, for example, *Maitrī Upaniṣad* 1.3, *Manusmṛti* 6.76-77, and *Dhammapada* 150.

[14] *Palledārī* is the work of carrying heavy loads, a lot considered to be of low status and extreme hardship.

[15] One's "own *dharma*" or *svadharma* is specific to an individual and takes into account many relative positions, including gender, *varṇa* (one's caste and social status), as well as *āśrama*, or stage of life.

Every day carry on your religious regimen (*upāsana*) regularly in the morning and evening, and conduct your ordinary life and activities in such a way that you always benefit others. And if it is not possible to assist others, then at least see to it that you do not harm anyone else.

It is extremely essential to see Bhagavān immanent everywhere.[17] By seeing Bhagavān immanent everywhere, you cannot incur sin. Whatever sin one has committed in the past will also be destroyed. But see to it that you do not commit sin once you have started taking the name of Bhagavān, because any sins you do commit will be extremely difficult to free yourself from afterwards. This is because the sins that were committed earlier can be destroyed by a mere dip in the Ganges River; however, whatever sins are committed within the Ganges River, or within a holy place, those will be as:

[Sanskrit:] *bajra lepo bhaviṣyati* ।

Meaning it will be as difficult to remove as a line etched on stone. Hence, be fearful of committing sins while taking the name of Bhagavān.

If one follows one's own *dharma* and sings Bhagavān's hymns, then all the sins from one's previous births will be cut away, and experiencing happiness and peace, one will gain salvation (*sadgati*).[18]

---

[16] To remember God can refer to continuously chanting the name of God.

[17] See, for instance, *Bhagavad Gītā* 4.35 and 6.29-30.

[18] *Sadgati* means a better path, or a better life; in this context, salvation in the afterlife.

## *Teaching #3*

**Man has freedom in action, but enjoying their fruits is in the power of another**[19]

Therefore, do those actions (*karma*) that yield the best fruits.

ॐ

A thief is free to steal, but the court will determine his reward; whatever the court may decide, that is what he must endure, whether he likes it or not. Man, similarly, can act however he wishes. He can perform virtuous acts, for which he will be sent to heavenly realms and enjoy divine pleasures, or conversely, he can perform evil acts, for which he will earn hells such as Raurava and suffer extremely fearsome and sorrowful results.

Human birth is considered to be a birth of action. Here [on earth] man is free to act, meaning that it is possible to take whatever action we wish. If man wishes, he can even directly meet the omnipotent—Being, Consciousness, and Bliss—Paramātmā.

Man must reap the fruits of his actions. It is impossible to escape the fruits of whatever actions he performs. Yes, this is a certainty:

[Sanskrit:] *dharmeṇa pāpamapanudati*[20]

---

[19] See *Bhagavad Gītā* 2.47, *karmaṇy evādhikāras te mā phaleṣu kadā cana* ǀ

*mā karmaphalahetur bhūr mā te saṅgo 'stv akarmaṇi*ǁ *"You have control over action alone, never over its fruits. Live not for the fruits of action, nor attach yourself to inaction."*

[20]*Mahānarāyaṇa Upaniṣad*, Chapter 22 verse 1.

By performance of *dharma*, evil is destroyed. Hence, if someone does commit a sin sometime, he should perform meritorious acts to destroy them. As merit increases, sin decreases. That's why they say,

[Sanskrit:] *japato' nāstipātakam*

By repeating (*japa*) the *mantra* of Bhagavān's name, sin is destroyed.[21] Hence, if someone has committed an evil deed or non-prescribed act and wants to free himself of all demerit, then he should begin meritorious actions full of faith and devotion, and to the best of his abilities, he should chant the name (*mantra*)[22] of Bhagavān. By doing so the past demerit will gradually be destroyed, and within a short time, he will fill in the pit[23] and henceforth, pure fruit will begin to accumulate,[24] through which he will reach salvation.[25]

Even if one remembers Bhagavān unintentionally, one's sins will be destroyed. This is just like a fire, which burns whatever it touches despite having no conscious intention. The significance of this statement is that even as it is the self-nature (*svabhāva*) of fire to burn whatever it comes into contact with, in the

---

[21] This is the fifth verse of the popular "108 Names of Viṣṇu" Stotra. The full verse is: *anantam kṛṣṇagopālam japato'nāstipātakam* I *gavam koṭi pradanānasya aśvameva śatasya ca* II: "By ceaselessly chanting the name of Kṛṣṇagopāla one cannot fail, and one will gain ten thousand cows and hundreds of horses."

[22] The term *mantra*, a powerful and sacred utterance, is in parentheses in the original.

[23] This is an imaginative expression of remedying a deficit, conjuring someone shoveling soil into a hole and then building up a mound.

[24] *Sañcita*, accumulated, is one of the terms used to describe the three types of *karma* possible by human endeavor.

[25] True path (*sadgati*), can also mean "good end" or salvation.

same way it is the self-nature of Bhagavān that any remembrance of him destroys demerits.[26]

The mind has deteriorated over countless births, so it is difficult to generate love (*prema*) for Bhagavān, but even with a sullied and faulty mind, if one contemplates Bhagavān, then one can obtain his favor.

There is one thing that needs to be understood here: however faulty the mind may have been in the past, however evil and sinful one might have been in the past, it doesn't matter. It is just not possible to continue doing evil when faced with the evil-conquering force that resides in the name of Bhagavān.

## *Teaching #4*

### Don't waste all your cleverness[27] on satisfying your stomach; the cleverest of all is the person who worships Bhagavān

No one can be saved by singing hymns. You do not serve Bhagavān by serving the king, nobleman, merchant or moneylender (*rājā, raī*, *seṭh*, and *sāhūkār).*[28]

ॐ

---

[26] See *Bhagavad Gītā* 4.37, *yathaidhāṃsi samiddho 'gnir bhasmasāt kurute 'rjuna* | *jñānāgniḥ sarvakarmāṇi bhasmasāt kurute tathā* || "As a blazing fire turns fuel to ashes, so does the fire of knowledge (*jñāna*) turn all actions (*karmāṇi*) into ashes."

[27] The term *cāturi* has the same meaning in Hindi and in Sanskrit: worldly cleverness or mental dexterity.

[28] *Rājā, raī*, *seṭh*, and *sāhūkār* is a list of four commonly wealthy and empowered social groups who often hire brahmin priests to perform religious activities, such as chanting devotional hymns.

Nowadays people consider themselves to be really intelligent. Yet all their cleverness is focused on their bellies; all their cleverness ends up in their stomachs. Their intelligence (*buddhi*) does not go beyond their belly. They devote all their time to bandaging the ulcers in their stomach, and thus their whole lives are wasted. In reality, there can be no greater loss than this in a man's life.

One must perform hymns (*bhajan*). One cannot escape from performing hymns.

[Sanskrit:] *sarvajña sarvaśaktimān kartumakartum anyathākartusamartha*[29]

If you do not serve that Bhagavān, then you will serve at the feet of the worldly ruler, the king, *rājā*, *seṭh*, or *sāhūkār*.[30] If we do not seek aid from the superior, then we must seek aid from the inferior. Therefore, the great-minded [person] will depend on Paramātmā who will assist one in both this and the other worlds. Regardless of how much wealth one accumulates, it will always be limited, and as one's currently manifesting (*prārabdha*) *karma* changes, one can become impoverished. So it is of little use to rely on a person whose own position is uncertain. The most clever of all is he who performs the hymns of Paramātmā, who can grant happiness everywhere in this world as well as the other world.

---

[29] Guru Dev does not translate this common phrase for his audience because it is readily understandable to his Hindi-speaking audience. It means, "He who is all-knowing, all-powerful, with the freedom to perform an action, or not to perform it, or to perform it differently." God is described as having three types of *śakti* (powers): *kartum*, *akartum*, and *anyathā-kartum*. *Kartum* is the power through which God controls the world. That which He wills, comes to pass. Despite being the cause of everything, God is also *alipta* (transcending or immune) from the world, which is described by the power of non-doing or *akartum*. Finally, *anyathā-kartum* is the *other* through which the impossible is made possible; through this power, God can accomplish what no one else can.

[30] Here Guru Dev appears to be addressing an audience of brahmin priests, who are commonly hired to perform ceremonies for such clients.

## *Teaching #5*

### Don't contemplate fulfilling every desire

For this bodily pilgrimage; act concentrating on gaining Paramātmā.

ॐ

Even the great ruler Daśaratha, a powerful wheel-turner,[31] could not have all his desires fulfilled, despite the fact that Bhagavān Viṣṇu incarnated in the form of his son (Rāma), and the divine king Indra gave him half of his throne. Unable to satisfy his desire to see Rāma coronated as king, he thrashed around like a foolish bullock and died.[32] When even great and powerful ones such as these cannot fulfill all their hopes and desires, then how can you people even hold on to the dream that your hopes can be fulfilled in sleep—much less the awakened state?[33]

The ultimate and mundane both go hand in hand, because by the very nature of *karma*, one cannot abandon (*tyāga*) it. If you were to abandon all *karma*, then it would be impossible to maintain the body. However, this insight must be maintained: for the embodied, besides those cravings that must be kept

---

[31] A *cakravartī* or "wheel turner" refers to a ruler whose power is so great that he "turns the wheel" of the world. Usually, this epithet refers to a being who rules through righteousness, that is, *dharma*.

[32] Guru Dev here alludes to the *Rāmāyaṇa*, the great Hindu epic about the avatar of Viṣṇu named Rāma who incarnates himself as the son of Daśaratha to restore righteousness to the world through the defeat of the demon Rāvaṇa. Rāma was forced into exile when Daśaratha's co-wife Kaikeyī pressed her husband to make good on his promise to coronate her son instead of Rāma, the elder son of Kausalyā.

[33] Hindu texts identify many states of consciousness. Here, Guru Dev contrasts the state of sleep (*svapna*) to wakefulness (*jāgrata*), and he argues that in neither state is it possible to have all of one's desires fulfilled.

to retain the body, one should leave behind fulfilling all other desires. In *saṃsāra*, there have been exceedingly powerful beings, but even they could not fulfill their desires. Therefore do only the required actions necessary to maintain the body, and concentrate your efforts on attaining Paramātmā.

The notion that the senses can be satisfied by enjoying objects of desire is like hoping one can relieve eczema by scratching. Worldly affairs are like coarse, knotted threads; if you try to remove one, the rest start to unravel. Therefore conducting the affairs of the world wisely, you should concentrate on the greater goal of enlightenment (*mukhya buddhi*).

## *Teaching #6*

**That which is fated (*bhāgya*) will undoubtedly come to pass and must be experienced; therefore, whether it be wealth or poverty, endure it courageously when it comes**

ॐ

A human being cannot sit quietly doing nothing. Through the mind (*manas*), intellect (*buddhi*), vital breath (*prāṇa*), and sense organs (*indriyoṁ*),[34] it is the human's self-nature (*svabhāva*) to act continuously. Each individual, according to his latent tendencies (*samskāras*),[35] naturally undertakes action

[34] The common *yogic* conception of the human body is referenced here, including *manas*, *buddhi*, *prāṇa*, and *indriyoṁ*.

[35] The term *samskāra* denotes the multiple impressions created by the thoughts, desires, and deeds of an individual which carry over into other lives as latent tendencies toward future action.

according to his own nature. Therefore the compulsion to act is natural (*svabhāvik*).

It is an established doctrine (*siddhānta*) that whatever one's action, so shall the fruits of that action unfailingly befall the doer. The fruits of actions done within a brief time are not exhausted even over a long timespan. Indeed, the actions done in one life cannot be fully exhausted in the next life. Unexhausted actions go on accumulating. As long as the collection of *karma* is not ended, the individual soul must enter the womb again and again. Therefore, upon attaining human birth, one should exhaust this store of *karma*.

The Vedic scriptures have categorized *karma* into three types and explained three means (*upāya*)[36] to exhaust each respectively. Accumulated (*sañcita*), currently manifesting (*prārabdha*), and amassing (*kriyamāṇa*)—these are the three types of *karma*.[37] Accumulated (*sañcita) karma* are endless. They cannot be exhausted by experience. The means to end them is by attaining knowledge (*jñāna*), or by undivided devotion (*bhakti*) at the feet of Bhagavān. Currently manifesting (*prārabdha) karma* can be spent only by experience; there is no other way.

---

[36] Viz., *upāya*, "skillful means," or "clever approach."

[37] *Sañcita* is the "accumulated" mass of *karma* from the past. That portion of the *sañcita karma* that influences human life in its present incarnation is called *prārabdha*, that which is "currently manifesting," and which produces the human body. *Sañcita karma*'s influence can be seen in each human's character, for our tendencies, aptitudes, capacities, and inclinations are affected by the actions we took during past lives. *Prārabdha karma* is not destroyed by knowledge and must be experienced. *Kriyamāṇa karma* is that which is "being made" in this lifetime or presently being created and added to *sañcita karma*. While some *kriyamāṇa karma* may bear fruit in the current life, others do not and are stored for future births. *Kriyamāṇa karma* is also called *āgamī*, coming or arriving. Like *sañcita karma*, once true knowledge of the falseness of agency dawns, this type of *karma* does not produce bondage.

[Sanskrit:] *avaśyameva bhoktavyaṁ kṛtaṁ karmaṁ śubhāśubham* I [38]

By dedicating your actions to Bhagavān, there will be no cause for bondage. In this fashion, having burnt up accumulated (*sañcita) karma* through the fire of knowledge, currently manifesting (*prārabdha) karma* by experience, and amassing (*kriyamāna) karma* by dedicating them to Bhagavān, one is freed (*mukta*) from *karma* bondage, which is thus called *mokṣa*.

If you are stymied on attaining knowledge due to lack of spiritual practice (*sādhana*),[39] then at the very least you should start dedicating your ongoing actions to Bhagavān. By so doing, at least the actions done in this life will not be the cause of bondage in the future. In addition, you should keep in mind that currently manifesting (*prārabdha) karma* sets into motion results the experience of which even a sage (*jñāni*) cannot escape. Hence, the unhappiness that results from currently manifesting (*prārabdha* ) *karma* must be faced boldly. One should not lose courage even in calamitous times. Similarly, do not become negligent when enjoying happy occasions. By acting in this way, merit will accumulate, and you will win both this world and the next.

---

[38] Brahmananda Saraswati leaves untranslated this Sanskrit phrase which means, "Invariably, a deed done must be experienced, whether auspicious or inauspicious."

[39] Guru Dev here refers to those persons who cannot take the vow to perform *sādhana*, a disciplined spiritual regimen.

# Teaching #7

**Having attained human birth, don't waste it**

Understand and set out on the path of good fortune (*kalyāṇa*).[40]

ॐ

Do not waste precious time by dwelling on the pleasures of the senses—speech, touch, form, taste, and smell—or worry about your belly. You have been chasing these senses in previous lives as animals, birds, as well as insects. Even after becoming a human being, if you carry on like this, you will remain trapped within the 8,400,000 life-forms,[41] and attaining release will be difficult. Value your human birth! Act with discrimination. Understand your truly beneficial path, and behave in such a way that you need not continually return to the prison of the womb.

Commit your life to the *dharmik*. Submitting to the bondage of *dharma* yields fortune. Despite having freedom of will,[42] do not think, "We will not stay in the *dharma* system." If you stay in the *dharma* system, then it will better you in this world and even elevate you in the other world (*paraloka*).

If you think you are free of the system of *dharma*, then you will be ensnared by the system of *adharma*, and will ultimately destroy yourself. Mind

---

[40] *Kalyāṇa* conjures a complex of positive associations, including happiness, welfare, good, good fortune, and auspiciousness.

[41] "Eighty-four *lakh*" (a *lakh* is a measure of 100,000) is a common allusion to an infinite number.

[42] I have translated *svatantra* or "one's own devices" as having "freedom of will." Brahmananda Saraswati contrasts *svatantra* with *dharma ke tantra* and *adharma ke tantra*, which I translate as *dharma system* and *adharma system.*

your own *dharma*. Minding one's own *dharma* is verily the one means by which human life can be fulfilling.

Minding one's own *dharma*[43] is urgent in all the fields of one's individual life — personal, social, political, national, and international. In all areas, if one maintains his body, senses, mind, and intellectual health according to *dharma*, he can avoid *adharma*.

Neglecting *dharma* means adopting *adharma*. In whatever field one neglects *dharma*, in that [very] field *adharma* will take over, and that particular field will become sullied (*kaluṣita*).[44] Subsequently, all the fruits of *adharma* will befall personally on the offender alone. Only he who commits the action will be held accountable for the result. Hence, while carrying out any action—be it in the field of the personal, social, or political—consider carefully whether the deed is opposed to *dharma*. Do not execute even a portion of an action that is opposed to *dharma*. Sometimes actions which are opposed to *dharma* may be profitable to a man whose intellect is characterized by the quality of aggression (*rajoguṇī* ) or the quality of darkness (*tamoguṇī*), but their consequence will be powerlessness and disaster. This means that following *dharma* always yields merit,[45] and following *adharma* or the *dharma* of another (*paradharma*) is always disastrous.

---

[43] The concept of *svadharma* or one's own *dharma* reflects the personal situation of gender, caste, and stage of life.

[44] *Kaluṣita* can mean "profane, sinful, polluted, dirty, or black."

[45] More literally, "following *dharma* is always productive of auspiciousness" or *kalyāṇakārī*. The teachings of *Bhagavad Gītā* 2.31, 3.35 and 18.47 assure the listener that following one's *svadharma*, one's own *dharma*, even if faulty, is preferable to following the *dharma* of someone else.

# *Teaching #8*

## Mokṣa Arises From Karma

Each person can cross the ocean of being by resorting to desireless *karmayoga*.

ॐ

*Niṣkāma karma* does not mean that one must do actions "without any desiring whatsoever," because no impulse (*pravṛtti*)[46] is even possible without desiring. There are two causal factors to an impulse (*pravṛtti*)—one is the knowledge of *iṣṭa sādhana*, which means that one knows that carrying out a particular action will fulfill a desire; and the other is the knowledge of *kṛta sādhyatā*, which means that one knows that one is capable of accomplishing the action itself. Only by knowing both these things will a person have an impulse to act. If even one of these two is in doubt, the impulse to act will not occur. Thus, desire must precede an impulse. Hence, the resulting meaning of *niṣkāma karma* is that it is action that is done which is dedicated to Bhagavān. Action done for the sake of Bhagavān is verily called desireless action. Action surrendered to Bhagavān is not a cause of bondage. You have the authority (*adhikāra* ) only to perform actions; do not desire the fruit. Because the individual soul (*jīva*) has been experiencing such hardship over the span of millions of births, it simply has no discrimination as to what it should request. Consequently, when it does beg, it asks relative to its own level. Thus if the individual soul desires to get a specific result, it will desire something that affords a very simple result; however, if one leaves the [fruit] up to Bhagavān, who is omniscient and omnipotent, Bhagavān

---

[46] *Pravṛtti*, impulse, is a "turning toward" action.

will raise the level of the result to his height, and thus bestow a far greater outcome.

The man who acts mindfully, ever devoted to Bhagavān, attains the abode of Bhagavān, and in accordance with law, he attains heaven (*sālokya),* proximity [to the divine] (*samīpya*), and release (*mukti*), forever freed from the bondage of life and death. The means to obtain release is by performing *karma* itself, yet freed from the bondage of *karma.*

## *Teaching #9*

### The true meaning of life is to advance oneself for the future

ॐ

In comparison with the efforts worldly (*samsāri*) people take to gain wealth, children, and fame, they spend no effort whatsoever to become Bhagavān's devotee and wise. Such people neglect the discipline which yields greatest happiness, and instead grasp the discipline leading to sorrow. Happiness cannot come from a worldly object. The desire to obtain happiness from worldly objects is like trying to marry the son of a barren woman: since no barren women has a son, how could he be married? When there is no real happiness in worldly objects such as wealth, women, progeny, and so forth, then how can we obtain happiness from them? Our intelligence has indiscriminately grasped the undesireable rather than the desireable.

The meaning of life is to advance onself for the future. "If just filling and emptying your stomach is all there is,"[47] then human life is meaningless, so it is believed. If you live only to "fill your belly in the morning and empty it by the evening," then living is useless. You keep desiring to live because you have not yet had a vision (*darśana*) of Bhagavān: the purpose of life is to perform *sādhana* for attaining [that vision].

When seeds are roasted, they cannot sprout later. Similarly, when the human mind is roasted in the fire of knowledge and devotion, then there is no chance for it to germinate anew in the cycle of life and death. Therefore, try to become a devotee and knower. But don't become that type of knower who mutters, [Sanskrit:] *Śivohaṁ*, *Śivohaṁ*, *oṁ*, *oṁ*, and *ahaṁ brahmāsmi,*[48] and yet retains love for *saṃsāra* in wealth, women, progeny, and so on. Such superficial knowledge produces more harm than benefit. When people keep calling themselves *Brahman* yet stray from *dharma* and *karma*, they lack sufficient strength to remain in that state. Therefore, until the love for worldly objects is abandoned, do not fall into the trap of *Brahman*, and you should develop devotion to Bhagavān. Continually practicing devotion, when intense desire (*rāga*) for Bhagavān appears, then you will be released from the cycle of birth and death.

---

[47] A Hindi proverb, *yadi jholī bharanā aur khālī karanā itanā hī hai* ||. Many popular hymns attributed to Guru Nanak and other devotionalist [*bhakti*] poet saints urge people to find more to life than mere sustenance.

[48] Brahmananda Saraswati does not translate the Sanskrit, "I am Śiva, I am Śiva, oṁ, oṁ," and "I am *Brahman*." He here satirizes would-be knowers of Non-dual, Advaitin philosophy, who although still attached to *saṃsāra* chant famous *mantras* privileged by Advaitin philosophy identifying the human with the great *yogi* god, Śiva, and with the ultimate principle, *Brahman*.

# *Teaching #10*

## Suffering At the Time of Death

ॐ

The suffering one must undergo at the time of death is many times greater in intensity than the suffering that occurs at the time of birth. In the scriptures it is said that the great suffering at the time of death can be as intense as the stinging of thousands of scorpions at once. To bear the sting of one scorpion alone is quite difficult. Just imagine the experience if one were stung by thousands at once! Thus one can imagine the pain at the time of death.

Along with the suffering of birth and death, during one's lifetime one must undergo endless suffering. Without the realization of Īśvara, it is impossible to free oneself from this (suffering). As long as one has delusion (*moha*) towards *saṃsāra*, one must return to *saṃsāra* again and again. Delusion emerges because of impure mental states.[49] Hence, one should first replace all impure desires (*vāsanā*) with pure desires, and then one should strengthen the sole desire to realize Īśvara.[50] This desire must become so intense that no other desire can arise before it.

---

[49] Impure mental states, *aśuddha bhāvanās*, are at the root of attachment to the world. Brahmananda Saraswati seeks to press home the realization that life is suffering and attachment and delusion toward the world must be addressed by changing desires.

[50] *Īśvaraprāpti*, obtaining or reaching God.

## *Teaching #11*

**Let not the last days of life be spoiled**

ॐ

It is generally seen that whatever one worries about or practices for a long time is that which is remembered at the time of death. If a Vedic scholar goes mad, even in madness he will repeat the verses of the Veda. In the same way, during the throes of death, one will be unable to come to one's senses. At that time, it is highly probable that one will remember that which one practiced during life. Whatever mistakes that were committed in the beginning of life are already past, but not so future mistakes at life's end. It is said, "all is well that ends well"; in order to avoid mistakes at the time of death, begin right now to prepare for it. This is prudence. [51]

## *Teaching #12*

**Seeking happiness from that which you will be parted is a great mistake;**

If you love this world and its objects too much,

you will weep lifetime after lifetime

ॐ

---

[51]Some Asian texts teach the belief that the last thought at death determines the next birth. Here Brahmananda Saraswati notes that people can prepare themselves against negative thoughts and actions at death by making proper thinking and behavior a habit.

All of us here are related as boats in a river. Wherever you find yourself, in whatever condition, act wisely. Everyone here has his own "program."[52] If you probe deeply, then you'll realize there is nobody who can really be called a friend. One sees that there is always a case of "me" and "mine." In reality, in this *saṃsāra*, when one's own state is unclear, how can one assist another? All life is transitory, like a drop of water on a leaf. Wherever one has taken birth according to his past *karma*, there he must bide his time and practice *dharma* while remembering Bhagavān. By all means, perform all necessary actions, but perform them wisely so that they do not become obstacles along the path to the other world. Wisdom is that which enhances both this world and the next. To gain wealth by cheating someone is not wise, and is in fact foolish. Can one who is unclear about his own future ever be called wise?

Our advice here is don't cheat, even if you are cheated. Depend on your *dharmik karma*. Do not depend on cleverness and dishonesty. Act in *saṃsāra* in such a fashion that the work here goes on and the next life is also enhanced. This is possible only if you continue with your own duties and continually remember Bhagavān. If you act in this way, you can free yourself from the bondage of birth and death and be liberated from this body of urine and excrement. Otherwise, you must keep returning here.

You will eventually be separated from all objects of *saṃsāra*. These objects, from which separation is inevitable, are not worthy of being loved. Furthermore, it is unnecessary to love them. If you love them, you will weep, not only crying in this life, but crying in many lives to come. There is a story illustrating this point.

---

[52]The English term "program" is in the original.

Once Maharishi Nārada went to a village.[53] A local merchant treated him generously as his guest. Seeing his faith and devotion, the sage drank a glass of his milk. The merchant inquired, "O Maharaj,[54] from where have you come?"

Nārada replied, "From Heaven."

The merchant inquired, "O Maharaj, where will you be going?"

Nārada replied, "After wandering awhile in the mortal world, I will go back to heaven."

The merchant prayed earnestly, "O Maharaj, if upon returning you could take me to heaven with you, it would be a great blessing."

Nārada said, "Very good, we will go together." After a few days of wandering in the mortal world, the sage came back and asked the merchant, "Sethji, shall we go to heaven?"

The merchant replied, "O Maharaj, of course I need to go [some time], but my children are still young and innocent. They cannot manage our household

---

[53] Author Vettam Mani notes, "There is no other character in the *Purāṇas* occupying so popular a place in them as Nārada." *Purāṇic Encyclopedia* (Delhi: Motilal Banarsidass, 1975), p. 526. The *Purāṇas*, literally "old stories," were composed in Sanskrit, and appear over many centuries with great diversity. They detail no less than seven different births of the sage Nārada. In most tellings, it is actually Nārada who seeks release-giving knowledge from a god, but he becomes distracted by the appeal of the world, and only at the climax of the story is he reminded that his original intent was to transcend, not live on in, the world. See, for example, Mani, *Purāṇic Encyclopedia*, p. 528. Here in his story, Guru Dev positions Nārada as the wise teacher and a merchant as the student needing help in becoming unattached to *saṃsāra.*

[54] Nārada and the merchant address each other with respectful terms. Nārada is referred to as "great ruler," a common honorific for a learned person or superior, and the merchant or *seth* is addressed by his class/occupation, but with the affectionate suffix, "ji."

affairs. After a little while, when they are ready to take care of themselves, then I would like to go."

The sage left and then returned after some time had passed. He asked, "Sethji, now shall we go?"

The merchant replied, "O Maharaj, the children have now grown up and can now observe and listen to some extent, but they have not yet matured to understand complete responsibility. Next year let them be married, then I will surely go." After four years the sage returned and inquired about the merchant of his children who were sitting at the shop, "Where is Sethji?" The children replied, "O Maharaj, what can we say? Our father used to take care of the whole business by himself and since he left his body, we have been in deep trouble."

Using his divine [powers of] vision, Sage Nārada observed the whole scene and learned that the merchant had become [incarnated as] a buffalo. The sage went to the buffalo and asked, "O Sethji, now that you have left the human body, shall we go to heaven?"

The buffalo replied, "O Maharaj, you are so kind. I am ready to come with you, but I think that the other buffaloes in the household are all so weak, that if I don't pull the lead, all work will come to a halt. Moreover, some more new buffaloes are supposed to come. Until then, I'll carry on the work, after which, by your grace, I will surely go."

The merchant had given him a glass of milk with love, so Sage Nārada came back again after every two-four years to keep his word and return the kindness. One time when he came, he didn't see the buffalo. He asked the children, "Where is that old buffalo?" The children became quite sad and replied, "O Maharaj! That old buffalo was so very useful. It always led the others. Since it died, we've been unable to find another buffalo like it."

Sage Nārada meditated for awhile, and thereby learned in a vision that now the merchant had become a dog who was sitting and guarding his children's house. Sage Nārada approached the dog and said, "Hail, Sethji. What's new? Three lives have passed, now do you think you are ready to go to heaven?"

The dog said, "O Maharaj, you are very kind. I see your kindness on the one hand, and on the other, I see the laziness and irresponsibility of my children. O Maharaj! They are so irresponsible that if I am not here, a thief may come—even during the day—and steal from them. Therefore, I think that as long as I am around, I should guard them. After a few days, I will surely go."

After five or six years, Sage Nārada came back again. He didn't see the dog in front of the door. He asked the children and learned that the dog had died. After meditating for awhile, Sage Nārada saw this time that the merchant had become a snake, which was sitting in the basement guarding the family wealth that was stored there.

Sage Nārada approached the snake and asked, "Say, Sethji! Why are you sitting here? Has the time come to go to heaven or what?"

The snake said, "O Maharaj, these children have become such spendthrifts that if I were not here, they would waste it all. Therefore I think that the wealth that I have earned with such great effort should be protected; so long as I am living here, it would be best to stay here protecting it. Therefore, it is necessary for me to stay here, otherwise I would definitely be ready to go."

Sage Nārada left disappointed. Coming out of the house, he told the children, "There is a dangerous black snake near your treasure —it could harm anyone who came near it. Therefore, you should beat it. Hit it such that the stick doesn't crush its head. Just hit it on its body. Hit it so that it does not die, but [make sure] it leaves your treasury."

Listening to the orders of the sage, the children did as he suggested. They beat the snake all over its body with sticks, and then threw it far away.

Sage Nārada approached the snake and said, "Speak please, Sethji. Your children have beaten you up! Are you happy with that or not? Are you thinking of going back to that house and protecting their wealth, or will you now go to heaven?" The snake said, "Yes, Maharaj, now let's go."

The moral of this story is that if one starts loving one's home, children, wealth, women, and so on, then as long as we maintain bondage through such affection, we have to suffer millions of births. Therefore it is said, "Don't love *saṃsāra* excessively." If you love here, then you will be forced to weep for many births.

## *Teaching #13*

### Consider both friends and enemies with equanimity—both are conduits of your own bad and good *karma*

ॐ

No one is truly a friend and no one is truly an enemy. If someone is truly the friend of another, then he should always remain a friend. But this is not what we see. A person whom one considers a friend can become an enemy. No one is either friend or enemy by any inherent nature. Friends are the manifestation of our good *karma*, and when the fruit of our bad *karma* appears through the agency of a person, it manifests as an enemy. Happiness and sorrow both are the result of our *karma*. No one can give happiness or sorrow to anyone. Enemies and friends are merely the means through which the results of our good and bad *karma* manifest.

When the result of good *karma* arises, then all people appear as friends and they give us happiness. When the result of bad action arises, all people appear as enemies and give us sorrow. Happiness and sorrow are both our own property; you generate either one according to your own wish.

If I were to kill someone, I would be hung. The order to hang would be given by the judge and carried out by the hangman, but they would not be punished for killing me, because the punishment we receive is the result of our own actions. Therefore the judge and hangman are not responsible for my death, and I cannot rightly regard them as my enemies. Just as action is impersonal, so also is the consequence of action. The result automatically affects the conscious mind, which is the actor. Within the conscious mind, the mechanical result brings happiness and sorrow. From whomever we get happiness, remember that they are just the conduit of good *karma*, just as whosoever brings suffering are the conduits for us to experience bad *karma*.

Happiness and sorrow are always our own property. The person who becomes the means to deliver the consequences of our actions may mistakenly be seen as the cause for our happiness and sorrow. After fully comprehending this fact, we should free ourselves from attachment and aversion. When our own property is merely being returned to us, why should we blame another? If someone becomes the conduit of good *karma*, then let them appear. We should neither love nor hate anyone. Why love or hate a messenger? The main property of happiness or sorrow is ours; so why should we care about the carrier?

In sum, refraining from attachment or hatred toward anyone, we should experience peacefully the consequences of our previous actions, whether that comes in the form of happiness or in the form of sorrow, because both are our own property. Whether they are good or bad consequences for us, when they arise, we should welcome them happily.

# *Teaching #14*

**Confess misdeeds, but hide good deeds**

ॐ

By lying, the fruits of our sacrifices (*yajña*) are destroyed, and the benefits of austerity (*tapas*) are destroyed by arrogance. By insulting a pious Brahmin, the length of one's life is shortened. When we donate something and publicly congratulate ourselves for it in all the four directions, then the benefit of giving goes to waste. So what we wish to have destroyed, talk about; what we wish to preserve, cover it up.

If you commit a sin and then confess about it to another, its effects will be diluted. In the same way, if you perform a good action, and you brag about it, [so] its effect will be dispersed among the people who hear of it, and so its effect will be diluted

## *Teaching #15*

**It is false that one can keep sinning once one begins singing the praise of Bhagavān**

ॐ

There is no way that one can do evil on the strength of Bhagavān's grace. In reality, whoever worships Bhagavān with the attitude of *ananyatā*[55] will be incapable of non-prescribed acts.

*Ananyatā* means that for the [true devotee], there is nothing other than Bhagavān. Whatever actions the one who manifests this kind of loyalty in devotion takes will be only that which will please Bhagavān. In the name of Bhagavān there is a power to remove sin that is greater than any sinner can withstand. Vālmīki[56] and other sages are a good example of this. Before, they were very evil sinners, but they were able to leave their evil ways once they concentrated on devotion to Bhagavān and thus became good. However great a sinner one may be, once one starts worshiping Bhagavān, it is certain that one will attain the path of truth (*sadgati*).

---

[55] In the phrase *ananya bhāva se* the adjective *ananya* is literally "not other," or "no other." As Brahmananda goes on to explain the term, the noun *ananyatā* generally means the stance of seeing the divine without any other object, that is, seeing all as one essential divine reality, or unity. This closely aligns with *Bhagavad Gītā* 9.22.

[56] Vālmīki is attributed authorship of the Sanskrit *Rāmāyaṇa*, an extremely authoritative epic extolling the adventures of Rāma, avatar of Viṣṇu.

# *Teaching #16*

**If you want to serve Bhagavān, then follow the ideal of Hanumān Ji**

ॐ

Hanumān Ji performed all manner of service for Bhagavān, but never desired anything in return. If you adopt the devotional stance of a servant (*dāsya*),[57] then take the example of Hanumān Ji. Such is the true form of desireless bhakti.[58] Do that work inspired by [your] chosen deity,[59] and do not desire anything for yourself from its fruits.

One should work affectionately for your chosen deity. To preserve the happiness of one's chosen deity — this should be one's only craving. You should not act like this: after pouring a pot of water on Śaṅkar Ji,[60] then start asking for wealth, or jobs for your children, or for your wife to be cured of some disease, or a raise, or for your business to prosper. If you ask for such worldly things while worshipping your chosen deity, then even that deity will start to fear you; after all, everyone tries to avoid a beggar. That is why we should not demand anything from the chosen deity. Just continue to serve him. Should the chosen deity's attention become attracted toward you, and he has asked, "What do you desire?", even then just say, "I want your blessing, and that you please keep watching over me, nothing else."

---

[57] *Dāsya bhāva* is the attitude or stance of a servant to a deity.

[58] *Niṣkām bhakti* is a formal category of Hindu devotionalism in which the fruits of devotion are surrendered to the deity worshipped.

[59] The "desired one," referring to one's personally chosen deity.

[60] The god Śiva, the "auspicious one."

The result of desireless service to your chosen deity is purity of the heart and mind (*antaḥ karaṇa,* "inner organ"),[61] and the result of a pure heart and mind is awareness of reality. Therefore, the servant mood is very great. Just as fire is always immanent in wood, but becomes manifest only through friction, in the same way Paramātmā pervades the universe and only appears as a result of *upāsana*.

Do *upāsana*, but during *upāsana* do not demand anything. Make God become obligated, just as Hanumān Ji did. In the end, Bhagavān Rām himself had to ask, "Hanumān, you have done such service for me, how should I repay the debt?" This is how to make Bhagavān indebted.

In reality, Paramātmā can give much more than any individual soul can request. Should you make a request yourself, then you will ask for something minor in accordance with your own level, but if Paramātmā bestows, he will give from his level. He is omniscient and omnipotent; thus, anything is possible. Therefore, [if] you do your work and let Paramātmā do his work, you will lose nothing.

---

[61] The Sanskrit philosophical term, *antaḥ karaṇa*, is the "inner organ," often translated into English as the "heart." Since the inner organ is conceptualized as having agency and intelligence, it is also sometimes translated "heart and mind."

# *Teaching #17*

**Do not waste power (*sākti*) and misuse intelligence (*buddhi*)**

ॐ

Whatever you are going to do, think deeply about it before acting, because whatever good or bad that comes out of it will come back to you. The strength and intellect you have today are based on your previous actions. It is our responsibility not to waste power (*sākti*) and misuse intelligence (*buddhi*).

Through good behavior and following *dharma* we can make our worldly life happy, as well win a place in as the other world (*Paraloka*). If somebody chooses not to accept the existence of God (Īśvara), so be it, but if he wants to see any peace and happiness in *saṃsāra*, then he must understand all other living beings as he himself. In the same way, he should follow the principles of *dharma*.

A man learns from the company he keeps. As one's company is good or evil, so such things will be learned. It is a notable fact that on seeing his companions' behavior, a man does likewise; whether he is aware of it at all or not, he nevertheless acts accordingly. So the point is that man's actions and thoughts accord with the company he keeps. Therefore, if someone falls in with a bad crowd, then his actions and thoughts will be corrupted; moreover, those with whom he comes into contact will also sink. Hence, one should strive to associate with good company.[62]

---

[62] The phrase is "do *satsaṅg*." The term *satsaṅg* may mean a specific religious group (*saṅg*) of good or holy (*sat*) people, or the meeting which draws persons of similar religious stance in worship.

# *Teaching #18*

## As the deity (*deva*), so the worship (*pūjā*)

ॐ

As the disease, so the medicine; then there is benefit. An ordinary disease can be cured by ordinary medicine, but for chronic diseases, one needs to use special medicine. Humanity is entrenched in the impressions of countless past lives, and suffers from "world-sickness."[63] To free oneself from this terrible disease, one needs very powerful and great medicine.

The difference between a chronic disease and world-sickness is that a chronic illness spoils only one human life, but world-sickness keeps the individual soul wandering in various bodies, life after life, as well as causes the suffering in those lives. There is only one reason for the great suffering of the birth and death cycle, and desire is the root of the great terrible tree of world-sickness. Having taken root in the form of desire, it branches out vastly, and [feeding on itself], also nourishes the great terrible tree of world-sickness.

Life after life, this root is continuously strengthened. To uproot this takes a long time, until one can cut it down. Therefore, to pacify the desires of so many births, a long period of practice is necessary.

---

[63] The compound word here is *bhāvaroga*. The Sanskrit term *bhāva* comes from the verbal root *bhū*, "to become." Thus *bhāvaroga* can be translated as "sickness of becoming," "sickness of the world," or "sickness of rebirth."

# *Teaching #19*

**The false man can get no peace even if he is as rich as Kubera (God of Wealth) himself**

ॐ

Because of the absence of *dharma* in education, people's ability to discriminate between do's and don'ts has weakened. People think that whatever they are doing is correct. The belief, "I'll go to hell if I sin," has almost vanished. Because of this, falsehood has exploded in society nowadays. People seem to think that the meaning of life is to just attain sensory pleasures. Further, people have become unconcerned about the means by which they obtain the wealth necessary to have these sensory pleasures. Even so, it is certain *(niścita)* that engaging in wrong dealings for the purpose of earning money will never result in peace.

Lack of good company (*satsaṅg)* has increased characterlessness. Nowadays people do not believe they can manage without resorting to dishonesty (*beīmanī*), and they have no faith in the future or in Viśvambhara.[64] Have faith in Paramātmā, and conduct your affairs honestly. By doing so, you will feel satisfied in this life, and satisfaction is the true form of happiness. As it is said, *santoṣa paramaṃ sukham.*[65] A liar cannot be peaceful in this life even if he is as rich as Kubera. He will always be doubtful and his heart will burn [anxiously]. Thus he will not be happy in this world, and even in the other world, he will be ruined.

---

[64] "Viśvambhara" means "all-supporting," or the "support of the world."

[65] "Satisfaction is supreme happiness." This popular Sanskrit expression is found in many texts.

## *Teaching #20*

### Look for faults in yourself, not others

ॐ

The righteous person will experience peace in both this and the next worlds. He who acts immorally will not have peace in this world, much less the next world. Don't look at the faults of others; examine yourself, and discover the areas that are lacking and try to improve them. If you continually examine and improve yourself, one day you will be greatly benefited.

Never dwell on the faults of others. When we find fault with others, we pollute our own heart and mind (*antaḥ karaṇa*) in the process — this is not beneficial at all to us. When we ourselves are afraid of sinning, why make our own mind (*manas*) evil by thinking about the evil actions committed by another?

When we dwell on the faults of another, that person receives no benefit from it. On the other hand, those faults enter into our own mind and dirty it. So protect yourself. If you don't take care to protect yourself, then one day a storm will come and blow you away. Every evening, consider, "How many merits and bad impulses (*guṇa-doṣa*) came today? How many left?" If you continue observing your own faults, slowly, slowly, faults will begin to leave you. Think first about your own faults; to think about the faults of others will be very dangerous for you. Therefore, first protect yourself; only later, worry about others.

# *Teaching #21*

## *Saṃsāra* is not worthy of your love

"If you tie your mind to that, you will be cheated"

ॐ

This world is like a *dharmaśāla.*[66] To involve your mind here is a waste. Do your work in a simple way and keep your eyes on the journey ahead. It is foolish to trap yourself in affairs of this world. Whatever comes your way, deal with it appropriately. In this life of but four days,[67] it is not good to put on such a show. As long as you breathe, spend your time singing the praises of Bhagavān. Conduct your daily affairs courteously. Don't get caught up in too much thinking. If you allow your mind to get trapped in daily affairs, then again and again you will have to be reborn, wandering amidst the 8,400,000 life-forms. So act with great discretion; conduct your mundane business with the help of your body and your wealth, while keeping your mind in association with Paramātmā. Having compartmentalized yourself in this way, you can become happy and peaceful.

---

[66] A *dharmśāla*, "*dharma* house," is a retreat house or resting place, often built to house pilgrims at a temple-site.

[67] This colloquialism stresses the painfully brief human lifespan.

# *Teaching #22*

**Honor those who deserve honor, disdain those who deserve disdain**

ॐ

Mingling with characterless people is like listening to the *Gītagovinda*[68] or *Sūrsāgar*[69] from a whore.[70] If you drink water from the Ganges, take it from where the stream is clean; don't drink Ganges water flowing from a gutter. If a teacher is of good character, then listen to him. If you follow the words of a characterless person, it only serves to magnify your own lack of character.

The character of a Bhagavān devotee must be exceedingly good. You should understand that if someone is of poor character, he is not a [real] devotee, and is just putting on a show to cheat people. Save yourself from such deceitful people, and save innocent pious people from them.

Only he who is endowed with character is fit to be respected. A sweetmeat (*laḍḍū*) made of bad ghee will be crooked and bad; but when made of pure ghee, even its shape will be good. [71] If somebody declares that he is spreading devotional teachings of Bhagavān, then he should have an impeccable

---

[68]This Sanskrit poem concentrating on the great love of Kṛṣṇa and Rādhā was composed by a Bengali named Jāyadeva in the twelfth century. The *Gītāgovinda* remains one of the most famous medieval works of Indian literature, and its songs are still sung today.

[69] The *Sūrsāgar* is a popularly chanted and performed section from a sixteenth-century Hindi telling of the *Rāmāyaṇa* by the great Vaiṣṇava poet saint Tulasīdās.

[70] A *veśyā* is a prostitute or harlot.

[71] A *laḍḍū* is a round, slightly flattened and cream-colored sweetmeat commonly given to holy persons in tribute as well as to deities, hence the *laḍḍū* is associated with religious functions and behavior.

character. Only then will people know that through devotion to Bhagavān, all past sins can be destroyed and present problems can be overcome.

As a matter of principle, one should reject those deserving rejection and honor those deserving honor. If unworthy people are honored, then their number will increase and their stench will spoil society.

## *Teaching #23*

### Whoever has come, will certainly go; nobody stays here

ॐ

Always keep your bags packed. We never know when the call will come. The call of death is like an arrest warrant: there is no hope of further "appeal."[72] Then and there, one must drop everything and leave. Wherever, however, one must go. This need not be difficult if you are prepared from the beginning.

He who is always ready to go cannot commit sins. Sins are possible only when one forgets about the life hereafter. If one can always remember that he has to leave one day, then a man will never adopt lying and bad conduct.

Realizing that your fathers, grandfathers, and great-grandfathers have not stayed, it is easy to understand that, "I, too, cannot stay here permanently." Since it is certain that you will leave, then those people who prepare for the journey at the outset can rest comfortably; and if you are not ready, then you will surely have difficulty. Take care: "don't do something that will make you repent when you go."

---

[72] The English word "appeal" is in the original.

If you are not cautious, then you will be unable to save yourself from falling. The flow of *saṃsāra* is always downward. The tendencies of the sense organs (*indriyas*) always make man face outward,[73] and if you fall into the maelstrom of desires fed by the outward tendencies of the senses, then you will not have the capacity to pursue higher thought. Therefore, being cautious is imperative.

At the time of a man's death he will remember what he has done during his whole life, be it bad or good. Recalling the bad, sinful actions committed, and understanding the terrible result of all these actions, he will regret and become very sorrowful. Therefore, one should take care not to do even one sinful action that will be regretted at life's end.

## *Teaching #24*

**The more you give to Bhagavān in worship, the more you will receive in blessings. Any effort you invest will be returned to you many times**

ॐ

Worshiping Bhagavān is the one occupation in which there can never be doubt about losing anything. Worshiping Bhagavān is purely profitable. But the fact is that doing this profitable business must be fate (*bhāgya*). An unfortunate person will be involved in an occupation where loss is inevitable. It is a very great wonder that for wealth and other *samsārik* pleasures people work so

---

[73] In *Katha Upaniṣad* 4.1, Death teaches the young Nachiketas, "The self-existent pierced the sense openings outward; for this reason, one looks outward, not within oneself. A certain wise person, while seeking immortality, introspectively beheld the self (*ātman*) face to face."

hard—day and night, they work for that one thing alone. But to attain Bhagavān, which is so naturally beneficial, they make no great effort at all. They don't have time and energy to get to know Him from whom they can gain everything. How great is their lack of discrimination (*aviveka*)! What can be more astonishing than the fact that one doesn't focus on the very source of happiness and peace, the omnipotent Bhagavān, and yet struggles day and night to gain worthless worldly things? It is said,

[Hindi] "If you do one thing [properly], then all will come, but if you start with all, then all will flee."[74]

By knowing the one Bhagavān, you can readily gain everything. If you ignore Bhagavān and try to gain something [on your own], you will achieve nothing, and even if you do acquire something, you will not be satisfied with it.

If you ignore the real, [you] desire to catch the shadow, [but] if you catch the object of that shadow, then you'll immediately catch the shadow as well. If you chase after a shadow, the faster you run, the faster it will run away from you. That is why running after shadowy wonders and luxuries of *saṃsāra* is so foolish. If you catch the real nature of Paramātmā [on the other hand], then all this will automatically come under your command. Remember always that in worshiping Bhagavān, there is only benefit. Whatever time you devote to this will be returned to you with interest.

---

[74] This is a famous proverb: *Ekahi sādhe sab sadhe, sab sādhe sab jāya* || To become adept in any activity, one must first learn to concentrate. Trying to focus on too much will result in nothing, whereas by attaining complete competence over a single endeavor, one can build up to true mastery. This proverb is commonly used to encourage classical Hindusthani music students to master one *rāga*, which serves as the foundation for others.

# *Teaching #25*

## Paramātmā is Viśvambhara

He will take care of all your needs: don't forget him and become an ingrate

ॐ

The One who has created you is omnipotent, and his name is Viśvambhara. He has taken upon himself the care and sustenance of the universe. Have faith in Him — he will protect that which he has created. But if you forget him, you commit the fault of ingratitude, and then it is no wonder if He neglects you.

[Sanskrit:] *kā cintā mama jivane yadi harirviśvambharo gīyate* ।

*nocedarbhaka jīvanāya jananī stanyaṃ kathaṃ nissaret?*॥ [75]

If Bhagavān's name is Viśvambhara (the doer of maintenance and sustenance), then it is futile for me to worry in this life about how to fill my stomach. Doubting Paramātmā's ability to provide sustenance is like asking how is it that a mother has milk in her breasts even while the child is still in the womb?

There cannot be a more shining example than this of Paramātmā's capacity to care for us all: even before the enjoyer emerges, the provision for his enjoyment is already provided. So have faith in Viśvambhara. The one who took care of you inside the womb will continue to take care of you even now. Don't forget him.

---

[75] Guru Dev's translation that follows is a close and fairly literal translation.

# *Teaching #26*

**Live the days of your life peacefully and without wasting time making a fuss**

ॐ

Even great emperors such as Daśaraṭha[76] could not fulfill all their desires. Hence it is a complete blunder to try to fulfill all the desires that may arise in one's mind.

One should not forget that one day it will be necessary to leave this place. Whatever the "program,"[77] it will only continue here. What's there remains as it is. The journey must commence alone, without taking anything from here. Therefore, you should not trouble yourself much for the things that you have to leave one day. As long as you live, live peacefully. When it is certain that all things cannot be completed, then it is foolish to make a great fuss about them. Doing your own *dharma* and duties peacefully, remember Paramātmā.

Viśvambhara is the creator. He protects, and he himself manages all things. But if you do not have faith in Him, and instead place your faith on cleverness, deceit, and dishonesty, then your whole life will be unpeaceful, and the path ahead will be dark. So act in such a way that you experience peace in this life, and your future path will be bright, too.

---

[76] Father of Lord Rāma.

[77] The English word "program" is in the original.

## *Teaching #27*

### Gain Power (*Śakti*),[78]

A life without power is wasted

ॐ

Become powerful and live out your life. You have obtained a human body, so pursuing the aims of man,[79] become strong. Remember that you are the descendant of those maharishis who could do anything in *saṃsāra*. Yet even though you descend from those who could create another world themselves at will,[80] you are now surrounded on all four sides by misery and lack of peace. If you have forgotten the treasure that is hidden in your own house, then you can only go begging from door to door.

What a shame it would be were a tiger to join a herd of sheep, start bleating, "baa, baa,"[81] and then begin thinking he was actually happy. In the same way, what a great fall if a citizen of Bharata (India) forgets his own ancient spiritual and divine heritage, and starts thinking that happiness and contentment comes from obtaining worldly things such as superficial words, touch, form, taste, and smell.

---

[78] The term here is *śakti*, "power." *Śakti* has religious tones, since it can mean the spiritual power one develops through faith and austerities. When used as a personal noun, it refers to a goddess or goddesses in the plural, or the Great Goddess conceptualized as "Power."

[79] The concept of the great ends of mankind, or *puruṣārtha*, is generally understood to be fourfold: pleasure (*kāma*), worldly gain (*artha*), *dharma*, and *mokṣa*.

[80] This refers to stories about sages such as Viśvamitra, who once created an alternative heaven for the king Triṣaṅku, and is meant to illustrate their awesome powers. The onomotopoetic sound in Hindi is "bheṁ, bheṁ."

[81] The onomotopoetic sound for the bleating of sheep in Hindi is "bheṁ, bheṁ."

To become powerful, recall the examples of your forefathers. Enter the shelter of the omnipotent controller of creation.[82] Develop your spiritual powers. Earn the authoritative power over the creative principle of the controller of creation.[83] Only then can you become powerful in reality, and a firm, powerful force. Remain convinced that even today you can be a knower of past, present, and future, and you can make all the elements and powers of the universe favorable to you. Your birth took place in Bharata. Unlimited powers reside within you. Strive to manifest them and become powerful, with head held high.

## *Teaching #28*

**Don't get involved in the controversy[84] over form or formlessness**

ॐ

That which is without form is with form. Like a calm ocean, it appears to rise up in the form of waves. Just like we understand a "wave" to be that which appears to emerge from the surface of the ocean, and [subsequently] merge with the ocean on its descent, in just such a way the *nirguṇa*, *nirākāra*, all-pervading Paramātmā takes form, *saguṇa*, *sākāra*.

We say that the very appearance of Bhagavān in a *sākāra* form is the direct proof of the existence of *nirākāra*. Fire is immanent everywhere in wood,

---

[82] The specific term used here is *sarvaśaktimān jaganniyantā*.

[83] The specific term used here is *jaganniyāmikā cetanā sattā*.

[84] One of the longest debates in Hindu philosophy has centered on whether the ultimate has form or is formless. In this lecture, Brahmananda Saraswati seeks to bypass the argument to enjoin his listeners to begin any meritorious spiritual path.

which is established in direct form when we rub some part of the wood and fire appears.

It is an established doctrine (*siddhānta*) that the *nirguṇa*, *nirākāra* is the *saguṇa*, *sākāra*, and from *saguṇa* and *sākāra*, the *nirguṇa* and *nirākāra* is made visible. Hence, don't get involved with or set your mind on debates about the formless and formed. By setting oneself on faith, great welfare comes. There is no gain in inciting debates about the *nirākāra* and *sākāra*, and the *siddhānta*.

Whether you place your seal[85] on *nirākāra* or *sākāra*, to the *nirākāra* and *sākāra* it will make no difference. For your own welfare, strive to develop faith in anything. Firm your faith in *ātma* or *Paramātmā*, learn the necessary spiritual exercises from some *satguru*,[86] and according to your eligibility, take up a spiritual practice (*sādhana*) once you understand the methods of appropriate practice. When faith in the *sākāra* becomes strong, then the bondage of life and death and will be cut, and [one will] lead a happy and peaceful life in this world as well.

---

[85] The English word "seal" is in the original.

[86] A "real" or "true" guru, that is, an authentic teacher.

## *Teaching #29*

### As the Costume, so the Dance

ॐ

Don't soil the seat where you expect to sit.

Whatever post you have accepted, don't degrade it. [It is best to n]ever consider any [position] as yours, but if you think it's yours, then whatever position you have accepted, take care of it appropriately. Whatever work you have taken in your hand, put your full energy into it to bring it to an orderly conclusion.

Apply your hand to that kind of work for which you are capable and interested. If you are only [attracted to] the grandeur of starting such work, then later when things get difficult you will have no peace. Therefore, do only that work in this world where there is the least risk of discontent. Always pay attention to this point: never bring disgrace to any post you have accepted. Maintain excellent relations with your mother and father, so that your position as son is not disgraced. Maintain loving, excellent relations with brothers and sisters, so that your position as brother is not disgraced. Maintain excellent relations with your wife, exercising proper limits, so that your position as husband is not disgraced. With your guru, be humble and worshipful, so that your position as disciple is not disgraced.

If you are working in a civil servant post, conduct your work legally and don't take advantage of your position and disgrace yourself in view of all the people. The gist is that whatever seat you occupy, don't soil it. In accordance with your birth, whether [you are a] Brahmin, Kṣatriya, Vaiśya, Śūdra, whatever your birth be in whatever family (*kula*), don't corrupt[87] the boundaries of that family. Whatever *āśrama* you have accepted, be it student, householder, forest-dweller, or renunciant, protecting the laws of each, perform it with dignity.[88] Don't ever act in such a way that the place you occupy and your position will be disgraced.

## *Teaching #30*

### Love (*Prena*) for Paramātmā, and for *Saṃsāra*, just the Shadow of Love

ॐ

Love should not be associated with things of *saṃsāra*. Activities cannot be stopped; all activity persists. As long as you have a body, you have currently manifesting (*prārabdha*) *karma*. Therefore, don't worry at all that if you abandon love for the world that you will be unable to carry out your actions. And this is also true: love is not distributed everywhere in the same way. Love of worldly objects and love of relations have different orders of magnitude. Therefore reserve your greatest love for Paramātmā, and your ordinary love for the activities of *saṃsāra*. Day to day dealings — meaning the experience of *saṃsāra* — will be taken care of by currently manifesting (*prārabdha*) *karma*; such work should be done just under the shadow of love. Since daily actions can be carried out with the help of a simple shadow, it is a misuse to employ that which casts the shadow. To deal with worldly affairs, if you make worldly goals their own subject of attachment, then you'll lose in the deal. It's a dangerous thing to keep

---

[87] He uses the term *bhraṣṭa*, which can mean "pollute" as well.

[88] The Sanskrit terms are used: *brahmacārya*, *gṛhastha*, *vānaprastha*, and *sannyāsi*.

this sense of "my-ness" with regard to wealth, son, and wife. If love grows within, then you will keep hanging in the [world of] *saṃsāra*, and your journey beyond will be dark. Therefore give your foremost love to Paramātmā, and keep just the shadow of love for your mundane affairs, so that your work here will not be disrupted and your future will become bright.

## *Teaching #31*

### To be born a human is more fortunate than to be born a god (*deva*);

### Make human life fruitful by fulfilling the ideal human goals[89]

ॐ

Taking birth as a god is considered akin to taking birth in any of the other lifeforms that experience living. Birth as a god is attained by those who perform certain sacrifices (*yajña*) and *karma*, etc. associated with divinity, with the intention to enjoy divine pleasures. The minds (*buddhi*) of the gods wander incessantly because of the abundance of enjoyable things in the world of the gods, and hence they cannot perform *puruṣārtha*. For this reason, the human birth is considered superior, because here the human being can perform *puruṣārtha* as one is capable, and by doing as much *puruṣārtha* as possible, the human being himself can directly obtain Parabrahman (*sākṣāt parabrahman*).

A human being is like a lump of pure gold, whereas gods are like fine jewelry.[90] Having been perfected as jewelry, [the gods] are completed; since their

---

[89] The ideal human goals, or *puruṣārtha*, are understood to be fourfold: pleasure (*kāma*), worldly gain (*artha*), *dharma*, and *mokṣa*.

progression is complete, they cannot be improved. On the other hand, as long as gold is in the form of a lump, its progress is limitless; it is capable of superior work, and it can be made into superior jewelry. Hence the birth of a human being is said to be the very best birth for action. Having entered [this state], one should not act carelessly. The best *puruṣārtha* should be done with care. Performing one's own *dharma* and duty and having faith in Paramātmā is the greatest *puruṣārtha*. Strive so that in this lifetime you may experience undivided connection (*abheda sambandha*) with Paramātmā. Having firm faith in the Vedas and *śāstras*, respecting the conclusions (*siddhāntas*) drawn from the Vedas and *śāstras*, keep company with the saints (*sants*), *mahātmās*, and the wise (*vidvānta*), so that your human birth will be fruitful.

## *Teaching #32*

**Worry about him — the one who can release [you] from all worries**

ॐ

One can attain peace and happiness only when one is free from all worries. If you want to destroy all worries, then you must understand the true form (*svarūpa*) of *saṃsāra*. When *saṃsāra* is understood, then the subtle

---

[90] Here Guru Dev draws on ancient imagery recorded in the Vedic scriptures that remain sufficiently current that he can expect them to be well-known to his audience. For example, *Bṛhadāraṅyaka Upaniṣad* 4.4.4 teaches, "As a goldsmith, taking a lump of gold, reduces it to another newer and more exquisite form, just so this *ātman* strikes down this body and dispelling its ignorance, makes for itself another new and more beautiful form such as that of the departed fathers, celestial singers (*gandharvas*), *devas*, or of Prajāpati, or of Brahmā, or of other beings." This *Upaniṣad*ic passage continues by explaining, as Guru Dev does, that howsoever one acts, so does one become.

impressions[91] of *saṃsāra* will be dissolved. Its true form is such that once one understands it, then one can never again generate attached inner love for it.

Numerous types of worries crop up because of our love for various objects. Worry is so terrible that even a man owning all possible wealth, fame, and influence still feels vexed.

[Sanskrit:] *citā cintā dvayomandhye cintā caiva garīyasī* ।

*citā dahati nirjīvaṁ cintā dahati sajīvakam* ॥[92]

Worry is considered more powerful and terrible than a funeral pyre, because the funeral pyre burns one who is dead, but worry continuously burns the living. Hence try to become worry-free. Only Paramātma, who is supremely independent, and supremely certain, is able to free you from all worries. Thus you should worry most about attaining him, and then all other worries of *saṃsāra* will be dissolved.

So continue to engage in worldly activities in *saṃsāra*, but remain aware that this is just a matter of worldly activity—it's not something to be loved. If your mind gets entangled with some object and then starts worrying about it, your whole life could be spoiled. Therefore, keep your mind on Paramātmā and continue to live good manneredly in *saṃsāra*.

---

[91] The term Brahmananda uses here is *vāsanā*. This complex term refers to subliminal inclinations and habitual patterns that act as driving forces, often unrecognized by the individual. *Vāsanās* are the results of subconscious impressions (*samskāras*) created through action.

[92] This humorous expression is easily understood by a Hindi-speaking audience, who know that the pun implicit in the expression plays on the fact that the only difference between the words *citā*, funeral pyre, and *cintā*, worry, is the sound introduced by the *anusvāra*, a diacritic used to mark a type of nasalization. Guru Dev's translation is almost literal: "Between the two — the funeral pyre or worry — the worse, verily, is worry. The pyre (*citā*) burns the non-living; worry (*cintā*) burns the living."

## *Teaching #33*

**He who must judge right and wrong is watching all your actions**

ॐ

Paramātmā is the dweller within (*antaryāmī*). He resides in the hearts of everyone at every moment. He is watching each and every action. No action can happen without his attention. To think while performing an action, "nobody knows about this," is to imagine Paramātmā to be blind.

If you have done something wrong and and have escaped detection by worldly human beings, don't think for a moment that nobody knows. He who must judge right and wrong is watching all your actions; you cannot escape his attention. You cannot escape the awareness of the one who dispenses the fruits of your actions, and who can do nothing for the person who has ruined himself. What enormous lack of discrimination to try to hide from [public] view. If there's anyone to fear, then fear the omniscient and omnipotent one. Do not perform any action that will go against his wishes (*ruci*). His wishes are the *Vedaśāstra*. Do not perform any such action for which permission is not given in the *Vedaśāstra*.

You can never commit a sin if you keep in mind that Paramātmā is present everywhere. By understanding Paramātmā as all-pervasive, you can become a person of character; bring purity into all your actions; cleanse your emotional state of mind (*bhāva*); and conduct your daily affairs in accordance with your own *dharma* and family standing (*svadharmānukūla).* Only then will your heart and mind (*antaḥ karaṇa*) be purified. As the purity of your heart and mind grows, your resolution is strengthened, your actions become firmer, and your faith in Paramātmā increases. All manner of auspiciousness will come from increased faith in Paramātmā. Therefore adopt that path as your own by which all manners of auspiciousness will be gained, both in this world and in the other world.

## *Teaching #34*

### Remain in the four mental dispositions and you will gain both this and the next world

ॐ

In the life of a human being, the gross body (*sthūla sarīra*) is not of importance — the subtle body (*sukṣma śarira*) is. The gross body is only a frame — its controller is the subtle body, the mind (*manas*) and intellect (*buddhi*). In accordance with however a man thinks, the sense organs (*indriya*) and body commit actions. It is therefore essential to manage the mind.

To purify the mind the author of the *Yoga Śāstra* Maharishi Pātañjali shared this skillful teaching (*upāya*), "one should maintain the mind in one of four dispositions: friendliness, compassion, sympathetic joy, and equanimity."[93]

With your friends, hold the attitude (*bhāvanā*) of friendliness (*mitratā*); with those younger or smaller than you or with those who are suffering, hold the attitude of compassion (*karūṇa*); with those who are more contented or who are wiser than you, or those who are better than you in some respect, look on them with the attitude of joy (*prasanattā*) in their good fortune; and with those who oppose or hate you, maintain a feeling of equanimity (*upeksā)*; you should not

---

[93] Guru Dev paraphrases in Hindi the first part of the Sanskrit verse from *Yoga Sūtra* 1.33: *maitrīkaruṇāmuditopekṣāṇāṃ* I The four states are *maitrī*, *karuṇā*, *mudita*, and *upekṣā*.

generate the attitude of enmity (*sātrutā*) or hatred (*dveṣa*)in your mind. In this fashion, by maintaining one of only these four mental dispositions, the feelings of envy, hatred, jealousy, and so on will never arise in your mind, and you will naturally continue to purify your mind. By acting like this in your daily affairs, no hindrance will occur, and by turning away from the impurities of the mind, desire for enjoying things will naturally be reduced, and then the mind, having become inner-directed (*antarmukhi*), becomes fastened on the praises of Bhagavān.

## *Teaching #35*

### Don't get cheated by pursuing *siddhis*.[94]

ॐ

Nowadays most people are searching for *siddhis*. They think, "I want to attain some kind of super-normal power." Very few people actually have these super-normal powers, but there are many people who get cheated through their greed to attain *siddhis*. Our duty is to be vigilant. Just like a watchman in the night shouts, "Keep awake!", in the same way, we, too, must caution people to beware of crooks. The watchman yells, "Keep awake!", that is his "duty."[95] But if someone falls asleep unconscious despite this [warning], it isn't the watchman's fault. He who sleeps is looted. The spiritual teacher (*dharmāchārya)* is a

[94] The word *siddhi* refers to spiritual powers. A person who has attained *siddhis* is called a *siddha*.

[95] The English word "duty" is in the original.

watchman. Doing the watchman's duty is our work. We must keep [disciples] awake and awaken others.

*Siddhis* appear in five ways: *janmauṣadhimantratapaḥ samādhijāḥ siddhayaḥ* || *Yogadarśana* 419.[96]

1) There are those individuals who from birth are endowed with *siddhi* (*siddhas*). They may have done some spiritual practice (*upāsana*) in their previous lives, but not enough to have merged with Bhagavān, so for those people with previous spiritual practice certain miraculous powers can be found from their very birth. This is the case with Jaḍabharata, for example, who was a *siddha* from birth: he did not need to hear, learn, or memorize to understand.

2) Many kinds of *siddhis* can be found through the use of medicinal herbs. When I used to live in the forests, on many occasions Kols and Bhils came and told me about the qualities of certain herbs.[97] One time a Bhil came and gave me a root that could scare tigers away just by displaying it from a distance. By using certain medicines, man can live for hundreds of years. Thus many kinds of *siddhis* can come from medicines. There is also a medicine that produces the power to fly in the sky when it is kept in the mouth.

3) *Siddhis* can come from *mantras*. Should a deity (*devatā*) of a *mantra* become favorable, it will perform according to its special capability. This

---

[96] Viz., *Yoga Sūtra* 4.1, "*Siddhis* arise by birth, [special medicinal] herbs, *mantra*, *tapas*, and *samādhi*.

[97] Kols and Bhils are groups of tribal people who dwell in the wild regions of the Vindhya and Himalaya mountain ranges.

undertaking of *mantras* is the true form (*svarupa*) of *siddhis*. Ordinary people may obtain some *siddhis* from forest nymphs such as *Karṇa-Piśācī*, and so on, or ghosts, wandering spirits, or trifling demigods (*chudra devatā*), and they will tell people about the past and present, or they may do some magic and pretend to be *siddha yogis*.[98] This is how they cheat common people.

4) *Siddhis* can come from *tapas* (aseticism).[99] Practicing *brahmacārya*,[100] fasting, and enduring austerities to attain God is called *sattvik tapas*, from which peace and satisfaction grow. *Tapas* done with the aim to attract, kill, deceive, or immobilize someone, and so on, is the form of *rājasī-tāmasī tapas*. This will not lead to peace or satisfaction, but will lead instead to greater non-peace and agitation, along with desire and anger, and due to the increase of these inner enemies, ultimately results in the downfall of the aspirant (*sādhaka*).

5) *Siddhis* can come from *samādhi*. However, such *siddhis* are impediments in the aspirant's efforts to become enlightened while living. [101] This is

---

[98] These are all different types of beings in lower realms. A *yakṣini* is a forest nymph, *karṇa-piśāci* is the name of a minor deity, and the *bhūta-pretas* are ghosts and disembodied spirits.

[99] *Tapas*—from the root verb *-tap*, to burn—are forms of asceticism that "heat up" the body and produce fiery stores of energy.

[100] Commonly understood today as the first stage of the religious path for the twice-born, *brahmacārya* is the period of study that involves chastity. Here the term denotes proper chastity.

[101] The goal for the aspirant in *Advaita Vedānta* is to become enlightened while living: *jīvanmukti*.

because *siddhis* can cause long-lasting effects, and if one does not use up these effects, then they can continue beyond this life.[102]

The important point is that it is not good to assume that just because somebody can show off some magical power that he is always a *yogi*. The miracles that *yogis* have will be very subtle, and the goal of these miracles is not to attain fame, money, or things from people. They use them only out of compassion with the attitude of performing the welfare of the world. By understanding these established truths (*siddhāntas*), people will be saved from delusion.

Perform the devotional praise (*bhajan*) of God. If you make yourself eligible (*adhikāra*) for *siddhis*, then the *siddhis* themselves will follow behind you.

What is the meaning of becoming eligible? That worldly attachments do not exist. As long as attachments for the world remain — whether it be for a son, wealth, women, reputation, or fame — one will be weak. There is a proverb that even God (*Khuda*) fears a beggar. If you cut off attachment to the world and increase attachment to meeting the one Paramātmā, then clusters of *siddhis* themselves will follow behind you; you do not need to search for *siddhis*.

You should choose the type of path that will not destroy your respectability. When there is a possibility that you can develop a direct relationship with the omnipotent Paramātmā, then it would be your misfortune if

---

[102] In the understanding of Hindu asceticism, the effects of *tapas* — here, *siddhis* — can be dissipated through usage. Thus, numerous stories tell of jealous and worried gods who deliberately trick fearsome ascetics who have amassed such reserves of energy that they may rival the gods in power. Conversely, because *siddhis* are so powerful, they can produce significant *kriyamāṇa* (newly amassing) *karma* that will be stored up for future births if enlightenment does not dawn.

you should instead go around chasing after some petty *siddhis*. Understand clearly that if you start running around after *siddhis*, then even if they see you from afar, they will run away from you. If you understand *siddhis* as an obstacle in the path of your spiritual progress and thus free yourself of the desire to obtain them, then suddenly you will find yourself surrounded by *siddhis*. The best way to keep *siddhis* under your control is to be continuously inclined toward Bhagavān and never have a desire to use them. This is the path of self-dependence (*svādhīnatā*). If you begin to chase after the *siddhis*, you choose dependence on another. Then you cannot be the master of *siddhis*, you will be called their slave (*dāsa)*. Therefore try not to be a slave of *siddhis*, but rather try to become a master (*svāmi*) of *siddhis*. If you become the slave of Bhagavān, you become the master of *siddhis*. By becoming the servant of Bhagavān, then all will do your service — this in reality is self-control (*svatantra*) and the path to self-reliance (*svāvalambī*).

## *Teaching #36*

### The unity of *jīva* and *brahman*

"Freedom (*nivṛtti*) from birth and death by selfless service (*niṣkāma karma)*, protection through righteous behavior"

ॐ

By removing the veil of ignorance, one can clearly experience the indivisibility of *jīva* and *brahman*. The difference between *jīva* and Paramātmā is like the difference between paddy and husked rice. As long as the husk is still there, it is called paddy, and when the husk is removed, it is husked rice. In this manner, so long as the *jīva* is in bondage with *karma*, it is separate from Paramātmā. On breaking the bondage to *karma*, it is none other than Paramātmā.

Although paddy is rice, even so, without removing the husk, no one can cook and eat it. Similarly, without breaking the bondage of *karma,* no one becomes *Brahman*, for example, by just reading Vedānta books and saying, "I am pure, I am purified." The purpose of the Veda and *śāstra* is to show the path of escape from *karma's* noose. If we surrender our original amassing (*kriyamāna*) *karma* to Paramātmā, then we can be freed from the cycle of rebirth. Even if not all of the husk is removed, if only a tip is torn off, then that act itself will make it incapable of sprouting. To take birth again is the sprouting of *karma.* A purifer[103] has the quality to clean water, but if you do not grind it and mix it into the water, then the water's filth cannot be removed. In the same way, however good *Sanātana Vaidaka Dharma* may be, if one does not put it into practice, then one will not be able to remove sorrow and poverty.

## *Teaching #37*

### Renouncing thirst and worshipping Īśvara makes happiness possible

ॐ

Whenever great disappointment arises from worldly matters, the impulse to turn to Paramātmā is born. Bhartṛhari was shocked when he learned about the infidelity of his wife. The examples of Tulasīdās and Piṅgala (Bhartṛhari's wife) confirm this [insight]: only when hope for happiness in this world is broken, do

[103] Literally, *nirmalī*, a common tree of medicinal importance in India popularly used to purify water for drinking.

people redirect themselves toward the ultimate good (*paramārtha)*. But still, how many fools there are, who, again and again, despite experiencing the uselessness of *saṃsāra*, [still] do not abandon demonic (*piśācinī*) hopes.

Ceaseless, careful thinking is imperative. If you think the lack of women, men, wealth, family, servants, and so on is sorrowful, then go and look at the lives of those who have had all these things. If they have found happiness from them, then you go ahead and try to obtain them, too. Whoever has all these things actually has more distress. Therefore, abandon thirsting. One will find happiness by abandoning thirst and worshipping Īśvara. Do not humble yourself before anyone out of the hope for happiness in *saṃsāra*, because happiness cannot be gained from any outside thing. The treasury of happiness is inside yourself. Whatever exists outside is nothing but sorrow.

Those people who think that objects of *saṃsāra* give happiness in due time come to realize this is a fraud. You cannot get water from a mirage. From a distance one can see water, and we keep running toward it to get the water. And this will be the same situation of people who feel "happy" from worldly objects such as wealth, women, children, and so on, since they eventually become worried about accumulating them. In all this, there is really nothing but worry for them.

If you want to experience happiness and peace, then don't search for worldly objects outside, search instead within yourself. The all pervading Paramātmā is the true form of happiness and his permanent abode is in one's heart (*hṛdaya*).[104] Therefore, search for him inside yourself. If you search for him within yourself, then you will find him quickly.

## *Teaching #38*

### Don't complicate your life by constantly making plans

ॐ

The world is but a *dharmáśālā*. You remain here for four days, then you go on your way. Don't become too trapped in the complications of managing your abode in a resthouse — only do that work which will let you move on. If there is a scarcity of something, then no one worries much about it — they think, "Well, I am in this resthouse for just two days, so some way or another I'll adjust a bit, and then we will be leaving." If someone begins to modify a resthouse to fit his desire, then he will spend all of his time rearranging, rather than achieving the very thing for which he came from his city or village.

You should think of this very world as a resthouse. Life last just a few days; you will not be staying here permanently. Therefore, don't take great interest in the management of this world. Take interest only in so much as is necessary to sustain yourself. You should always remember that however many elaborate plans you make, none of them can ever be fulfilled. Therefore, ensnared by the thread of hope you make schemes[105] in futility, thinking about

---

[104] See *Katha Upaniṣad* 6.17, *Śvetāśvatāra Upaniṣad* 3.20, 4.17, and *Maitri Upaniṣad* 7.7.

[105] The English word "scheme" is in the original.

them restlessly day and night, wasting time in the process and without any benefit.

However much managing you do in this world, there will always be something lacking. Therefore when some vanity can never be truly fullfilled, it is futile to initiate it. Pass your life in an ordinary manner, enjoined by the *śāstra*, and work for the [higher] goals of man (*purusārtha*) by which lasting happiness and peace can be attained. Performing primarily the goals of man to obtain Bhagavān, and regarding the attainment of worldly goals, keep this firm faith:

[Sanskrit:] *yadasmadīyaṁ na hi tatpareṣām* ।

"What is ours cannot belong to others." Whatever lies in my destiny will surely come to me, nobody can stop it.

Accepting this, do not become overly preoccupied in worldly affairs, and conduct your worldly affairs with moderation. Place your primary focus on Paramātmā. By acting this way, you will experience peace in this life, and you will make your future path bright.

## *Teaching #39*

### What is the purpose of Bhagavān's incarnation?

ॐ

In the *Gītā* [4.7-8], Bhagavān himself explained the purpose of his incarnation: "When *dharma* has begun to be destroyed, to protect the good people and to destroy the wicked, as well as to reestablish *dharma*, I descend at such times from age to age."[106]

One can ask, if Bhagavān is truly omnipotent, then he can destroy all of creation at his very whim, so why can't he protect *dharma* and destroy the wicked without bothering to incarnate himself? The answer to this is that by assuming an incarnation, to rescue *dharma* and *dhārmika* people, Bhagavān displays himself, so his fame spreads wide, and as they perform his praises, throngs of devotees become released. *Jñāna Yoga* is very difficult — it is rare for any among millions to be capable and authorized [to follow it]. *Bhakti Yoga*, on the other hand, is simple — and all humans are authorized [to follow it]. If God were not to take on an incarnation with form, then how would there be any publicity for *Bhakti Yoga*?

When Bhagavān assumes a shaped form, he is not forced to play in births for the purpose of experiencing happiness or unhappiness; he takes on a body because of his *yogamāyā* — just as an actor takes on various kinds of characters, and acts in ways resembling them without his own qualities being unaffected, so Bhagavān performs only as a role in a play.

---

[106] *Bhagavad Gītā* 4.7-8: *yadā yadā hi dharmasya glānir bhavati bhārata* ǀ *abhyutthānam adharmasya tadātmānaṁ sṛjāmy aham* ǁ

# *Teaching #40*

**With but minimal attention from the mind, mundane affairs can go on**

ॐ

The question can arise, without the constant attention of the mind, how can mundane affairs go on? The answer to this question can be seen in the miserly man, who while attending to his mundane affairs thinks his wealth to be the most important, and is always worrying about his wealth while he keeps on attending to his mundane affairs; in the same manner, while ever worrying about Bhagavān, you can carry on your mundane affairs according to scriptural injunctions — there is no doubt about this.

By drawing distinctions between our priṃary and secondary priorities, the answer to this question becomes clear. Furthermore, when the mind holds Paramātmā to be primary, then Paramātmā's grace (*kṛpā*) is obtained. Paramātmā is omnipotent. Just a little of his blessing (*kṛpā*) can make an individual life completely fortunate (*kalyāna*).

The omnipotent Bhagavān made this promise:

[Sanskrit:] *ananyāścintayanto māṃ ye janāḥ paryupāsate*।

*teṣāṃ nityābhiyuktānāṃ yogakṣemaṃ vahāmyaham* ॥[107]

---

[107] This is *Bhagavad Gītā* verse 9.22. I translate more literally, "But those who always worship me with concentrating on me exclusively—to them, ever fixed in devotion, I always attend to their spirituality (*yoga*) and protection." Guru Dev continues his exegesis of the *Bhagavad Gītā* passage. In *Bhagavad Gītā* verse 4:6, Kṛṣṇa explains to Arjuna that he incarnates himself because of "my *ātman māyā*," or own power of creation or mystery. In Guru Dev's speech, he uses the term *yogamāyā*, which conveys the *Bhagavad Gītā's* sense of *ātman* yoga, and which has a long history of interpretation subsequent to the *Bhagavad Gītā*. In its simplest sense, *yogamāyā* can be translated as the

This means: I will bestow yoga (obtain the unobtainable) and prosperity (protection of obtained things) to those who worship me with the attitude of single-mindedness. All mundane affairs (*vyavahāra*) come with yoga and prosperity. Yet despite the omnipotent lord being ready to take on himself the whole burden of caring for mundane affairs, even still man keeps worrying about them, and stays ever engaged in mundane affairs, thus deprived of greater purposes; what greater foolishness can there be?

Since Bhagavān has promised this, one cannot question how mundane affairs can continue if one sets one's mind primarily on Bhagavān. When you engage your mind on Bhagavān, your mundane affairs will necessarily go on, and in a most superior fashion at that. This is the established teaching (*siddhānta*) of the *Upaniṣads* and *[Bhagavad] Gītā*, and it is the experience of the devotes of Bhagavān.

There is a very recent story — perhaps forty or fifty years ago — not too long, that there was this constable by the name of Chunkāī Dās. This man's daily routine consisted of rising early in the morning, and after bathing, he would chant the *Rāmāyaṇa* for a while and then go to work. One day while reciting the *Rāmāyaṇa*, he became so absorbed that he lost himself until he became very late. The time for his shift had came and gone, and he only realized that he was expected for duty two hours past the time his shift ended.

So when he arose from his worship, he looked around and realized that the time for his duty had already passed. Filled with anxiety, he went to his post, and said to the sepoy on watch, "There's been a big mistake, I'm so late today

---

"mysterious power of engagement." In *Advaita Vedānta*, it is sometimes personifed as *Yogamāyā*, a female force/divinity who is the impetus of *Brahman*'s engagement with the phenomenal realm.

that my entire shift of duty is over; it must be very disturbing to you."

Then the soldier on duty said to Chunkāī Dās, "What's happened to you? Just now you handed over your charge of duty to me, and now you have come back and are talking like this; what has happened to your brain, are you all right?"

Chunkāī Dās replied, "No friend, I was so distracted in my worship today that in fact I am just now arriving."

Again and again the sepoy told Chunkāī Dās, "You just now attended your duty, and after completing it, you handed it over to me; before I came, you were doing your duty as usual. When your time was over, you gave over the duty to me, and yet now you have returned." After repeated confirmations, Chunkāī Dās realized that while he was absorbed at home in the worship of Bhagavān, Bhagavān himself had come and completed his shift for him.

Then and there Chunkāī Dās left his job. He said, "If my *isṭḥa* can take such pains to do my shift for me, then I will no longer work." After quitting his job, he went to Chitrakoot and started doing the *bhajan* of Bhagavān full time.

Many devotees have this exact type of direct experience, when Bhagavān has fulfilled all their mundane affairs himself. The Vedas and *śāstras* emphasize that this is Bhagavān's pledge: "whoever thinks about me with exclusive devotion, I will certainly take care of all their mundane affairs," and the experience of devotees verifies this promise. In spite of all this, if someone does not do the *bhajans*, contemplation, and meditation on Bhagavān, it is a most unfortunate thing for them, and what more can be said about it?

In summary, I tell you this: apply your mind primarily to remembering Bhagavān, and engage your body and all wealth in mundane activities only as enjoined by the scriptures — and both this world and the next will be splendid.

# *Teaching #41*

**If you want peace and happiness in both this world and the next, then take refuge in the omnipotent Paramātmā**

You will indeed get release, but you will also get wealth, fortune, and respect, too.

ॐ

Do not think that by the *bhajans* of Paramātmā you will only receive *mokṣa* — realize that from the *bhajans* of Bhagavān, you will get liberation as well as wealth and respect.

The reason for this is that by performing Bhagavān's spiritual practice, one climbs the first step of listening; the second step is singing the glories of Bhagavān; the third step is remembrance; and the fourth step is foot service, meaning contemplating the lotus feet of Bhagavān ceaselessly in one's mind. Lakṣmī fears the day and night servant of Bhagavān's feet [thinking], "let not Bhagavān's love for his devotee become too great."

A woman never wants her husband to love any one else. Therefore, to break a devotee's concentration on Bhagavān, Lakṣmī appears in the form of an obstacle as wealth, fame, respect, and prominence, by which she may ensnare him in this worldy trap so that he will abandon Bhagavān. Thus, Lakṣmī swarms around devotees of Bhagavān in the form of obstacles.

Today the wealth for which you worry and scheme about day and night, and on account of which you skulk about to obtain cash, fame and prominence, will come to you without effort if you but turn towards Bhagavān.

The path of liberation is verily the *bhajans* of Bhagavān, but if you want worldly treasures, then you should also surrender to Bhagavān. When a spiritual aspirant does *tapas*, then the Lord of heaven occupying the seat of Indra will become fearful and he will place right before him obstacles to his *tapas* in the form of many temptations; in the same way, to interrupt remembering Bhagavān, Lakṣmī brings before one worldly treasures. This resembles something you might do if a dog came running to bite you: if you toss him a morsel of bread, he will get distracted. In the same fashion, Lakṣmī tosses a piece of gold, thinking, "It would be good if this devotee leaves my husband and doesn't come back."

Remembrance of God not only imparts liberation, but will also jolt Lakṣmī. Therefore, do those actions that will maximize your profit. By this we mean that by *bhajans* to Bhagavān all the ends of life can be attained. When you begin attracting the attention of the omnipotent towards you, then what is not possible for you? In these times, people leave their houses and are pushed around at the homes of Seṭhs. They have faith in the wealthy, yet none in the Omnipotent. Thus they stumble from door to door.

Today *saṃsāra* is stumbling after him who has faith in Bhagavān. So if you must praise someone, praise Bhagavān, who will provide for both this and the next worlds.

Reduce your worldly desires and increase your love for Paramātmā. The use of a human body is to contemplate and set off on that path on which all manner of opportunities will be obtained.

## *Teaching #42*

**Nobody in *saṃsāra* wants your mind[108] — use your body and wealth to manage your affairs and place you mind on Paramātmā**

ॐ

Your beloved friends and kinsmen, and so forth, all want to fulfill their own needs. Nobody wants your mind! Go ahead and withhold from your son all the things he needs for his studies, and then sit beside him and tell him how much you love him. Do you think he will be satisfied? Don't provide your wife with the things she needs, and tell her that you always think of her and will never forget her. Do you think she will be satisfied?

Take your dear friend who wants your participation and help in some project, but you do not help him. Tell him, "I respect you with all my mind." He will say, "Please kindly keep your mind to yourself, please kindly try to do this particular favor for me instead."[109]

The point is that in *saṃsāra*, nobody wants your mind. Everyone here is a consumer of your body and your wealth. You, on the other hand, are forcing your mind on others.

Just remember that the same mind that nobody in *saṃsāra* wants, is the very same mind that can do the work necessary to help you reach Paramātmā. Hence, with your body and wealth conduct the business of *saṃsāra*'s bazaar, and

---

[108] The term used here is the Hindi word *man*, which like the Sanskrit *manas*, connotes both "mind" and "heart."

[109] The grammatical forms here are exaggeratedly polite, suggesting a tone of sarcasm and an attempt to make a humorous point.

keep your mind on the path to Paramātmā; this way the activities of *saṃsāra* will not be disturbed, and the path towards the ultimate goal will become clear.

It is wise to train your attention only on what is necessary. Don't entangle your mind in the things of *saṃsāra*. Worldly activities will continue by giving just a tiny bit of help from your mind. Keep the greater portion of your mind internally on Paramātmā.

Become someone who knows how to abandon this *saṃsāra* by engaging your body and wealth right here. To become someone who is never separated from Paramātmā, focus your mind on recognizing him as always being with you.

Pay the price such merchandise requires. For transitory affairs of *saṃsāra*, you should pay only your transitory body and wealth. But your mind is an abiding (*sthāyī*) thing that remains with you — even in the next world, it will remain with you. Therefore attach it to an abiding object. The most permanent is Paramātmā, who controls all the universe, who ever and everywhere pervades all; attach your mind to him. Only Paramātmā is worthy of your mind's attachment. There is no other thing like it in *saṃsāra* that can satisfy you when you attach your mind to it.

You people [know from] experience that you are always obsessing about wealth, women, children, or favored friends. But can you [really] keep your attention on any of these things? You cannot train your attention on any one place for very much time at all. If your mind were actually satisfied by wealth, or by sons, then why does it stray to another place? No, the mind can never stay on one goal; this proves that no object of *saṃsāra* agrees with the mind. [The mind] goes near something, believing that object to be good, but within a short time, it abandons it. From this it is obvious that no object of *saṃsāra* can satisfy the mind.

Thus, doctrine *(siddhānta)* thus reveals that in *saṃsāra*, no one really wants one's mind, and one's mind, too, is never satisfied with any *samsārik* object — in other words, the mind is not fit for the world, and the world is not fit for the mind.

When the mind attains Paramātmā, then it becomes fixed on it, [and] it will never desire anything else. Therefore, this is certain: that which is fit for the mind is [none other than] Paramātmā itself. Thus attach it to that which is fit for it

## *Teaching #43*

### If you want to escape ruin, free yourself from sin and build up your merit

Whatever human goals have been enjoined by the *śāstras* are meritorious and give prosperity, worldly improvement, and *mokṣa*.

ॐ

However much effort is required for a deed, then that is how much effort is required. However much merit is required to cross the ocean of existence, [then] crossing will be impossible without that much merit. If someone's thirst requires a large draught[110] of water to be slaked, but you give him only a sip, his thirst will not be quenched.

---

[110] The two terms used here are *ser*, approximately one kilo, and *chatāṅk*, one-sixteenth of a *ser*.

You can acquire merit *(puṇya)* by reading religious books. Reciting spiritual books (*dhārmika granth*) of the *Gītā*, the *Rāmāyaṇa*, and so on is meritorious. However, reading alone will not build up sufficent merit to cross the ocean of existence.

I am not denigrating the recitation of religious books. One should recite; but having recited, one's duty should not be considered finished. You must also try to apply [the truths] that are written there throughout your actions. Only then can it be considered useful, and merit can accumulate markedly. If you want to escape ruin, free yourself from sin, and do not pursue human goals opposed to the *śāstras*; free yourself from sin, and acquire merit — this is the way to improvement.

## *Teaching #44*

### Engage your mind in *saṃsāra*, but not so much that the higher goals (*paramārtha*) are impeded

My point is not that you people should break away from all things, abandon all your daily affairs, and apply yourself to *bhajans* of Bhagavān. Continue with your daily affairs, but do them in such a way that your daily affairs do not become ungainly and impede your main goal. If you engage your mind in *saṃsāra* more than is required, then you will incur losses each day.

ॐ

Apply only as much glue as necessary [to seal] an envelope. If you put too much glue on a small envelope, then the envelope will become messy from too much glue, and the mess will render it worthless.

Your mind is like glue, sticking fast wherever you put it. In daily affairs, the mind should be placed with great consideration. It is necessary to consider first how much something requires one's mental attention. The main point is that we should engage the mind least in *saṃsāra* and most in the ultimate goal.

Pay attention so that all worldly affairs [can] be done as close to the rule of the *śāstras* as possible, [even while] applying but a very small fraction of the mind to it. If you continually think of Paramātmā in your mind, then your daily affairs will become pleasant and the ultimate goal will also become bright.

## *Teaching #45*

**A devotee of Bhagavān cannot stay sorrowful**

Living in the deep jungle for many years, I have experienced the omniscient and almighty nature of Bhagavān. Even where no worldly amenities exist, all the necessary amenities are provided for the sake of Bhagavān's devotee.

ॐ

How can a prince experience any deprivation in his own kingdom? A devotee of the all capable Bhagavān, wherever he dwells in the three worlds, will live blissfully. Well, how can the all-powerful see his own devotee so sorrowful?

It is necessary only to gain the blessing of Bhagavān once, becoming not other (*ananya*) with him through one's faith, devotion, and trust in Bhagavān. Then Bhagavān himself will take care of everything, and it will no longer be necessary to appeal to him.

When a child is sick, does he have to pray to his father before he will take care of him? Of course not. A father cannot watch his son feeling sick without trying to cure the child's illness. Similarly, whoever Bhagavān adopts, who draws on his grace, Bhagavān will keep fullfilling all his needs without so much as asking. It is an experienced truth (*anubhūta satya*) that the devotee of Bhagavān cannot stay sorrowful.

## *Teaching #46*

### Before your kinsmen lose respect in you, turn to Bhagavān

ॐ

It is inevitable that in old age, when the body becomes frail and one no longer has the ability to earn money, family members and close friends will start neglecting you. But if you seek help from Bhagavān, then there is no need to depend on the help of anyone else. Even if all of *saṃsāra* turns away, then nothing whatsoever can be lost.

There is a saying related to this,

*jā par kṛpā rām kī hoī, tā par kṛpā kareṁ sab koī.*[111]

He on whomever Bhagavān's grace appears, will begin to find help from all sides, because Bhagavān is omnipotent. The person who becomes favored by even an ordinary king will obtain aid from all the people of his state. In similar fashion, for he who turns towards the all-controlling, omnipotent Paramātmā, then all the powers of the world will start working for his benefit.

---

[111] This poetic Avadhi couplet commonly sung in devotional settings is literally, "Whomever has Rām's grace, everyone gives [to that person] grace."

# *Teaching #47*

**Bhagavān's pledge to his devotees: "I am ready to do everything"**

[Sanskrit:] ananyāścintayanto māṁ ye janāḥ paryupāsateǀ

teṣāṁ nityābhiyuktānāṁ yogakṣemaṁ vahāmyaham ǁ[112]

ॐ

"He who contemplates me with unswerving devotion, I myself take care of his *yoga* and *kṣema*, meaning I will provide him what he doesn't have, and that which he already has obtained, I will protect." This is the pledge of the omnipotent Bhagavān. Have faith in this and apply your mind to *bhajans* of Bhagavān.

Nowadays people place faith in ordinary persons, but they do not place faith in Bhagavān's words. Place faith in the pledge of Paramātmā, who is capable of doing everything, and both this world and the next will become bright.

Consider how you are always thinking about the most insignificant things. While farming, you think about fertilizers, which is nothing but excrement; for something to protect your property from monkeys, you spread thorns. So given that a mind can stay busy thinking of just thorns and excrement, then it is surely no big deal if one spends a little time contemplating Bhagavān. The big deal is this — that the one who can fullfill all work, the omnipotent Bhagavān, is ready to grant the desires of his devotees.

If, in spite of all this, a man doesn't turn towards Bhagavān, then it is nothing less than a great misfortune, and what more can be said?

---

[112] *Bhagavad Gītā* 9.22.

# *Teaching #48*

## One should chant (*japa*) and meditate (*dhyāna*) every night before sleep without fail

ॐ

It is all well and good to perform worship, chanting, and meditation in the early morning each day, but at night before sleep one must without fail do ten to fifteen minutes of chanting one's chosen *mantra* and meditation on the chosen image (*mūrti*) of your favorite deity. Quick progress comes from such a spiritual program.

In darkness, with your eyes closed, sit and repeat your *mantra*, and meditate on your chosen deity mentally, with your eyes still closed. You should not envision its whole body, but rather its feet or face, feeling that your chosen deity is looking at you with an expression of compassion and affection. Sight (*ḍṛṣṭi*) of your chosen one's seeing is itself effective. You should therefore not visualize your chosen deity with its eyes closed. Meditating in your heart on your chosen deity, who is looking [back] at you with an affectionate glance, you should repeat your chosen *mantra*. By doing this, fixed attachment for the chosen deity will increase, and if the mind grabs fast onto the chosen one, then at the end, its vision will come without fail. On the strength of this, you will cross the ocean of *saṃsāra*.

## *Teaching #49*

**The one who is always immersed in sensory pleasures will never be able to do any work; the more you spend in good company, the more you will reject bad company**

ॐ

Land that is constantly flooded is not fit for any work. By damming the water flow, and controlling it, then the land becomes very fertile; in the same way, they whose sense organs are always flooded over with worldly objects become completely useless, and cannot achieve anything: they won't be able to help themselves, or help anyone else.

Contemplating worldly objects is much more harmful than enjoying them. If one enjoys objects within the limits set according to the *śāstras*, it is not very dangerous. But if from predispositions to enjoyment one instead always engages the mind in [thinking about] worldly objects, then the *antaḥ karaṇa* (inner organ) will become weak and mentally powerless; life will become burdensome, and both this world and the next will be missed. Hence, flee from worldly objects, but even more important, rescue your mind from attachment to worldly objects.

"The mind's victory is your victory, and the mind's loss is your loss." [113] If your mind is conquered by worldly objects, if your mind has been gripped by worldly objects, then your life will become subordinate to objects. A life of dependence on objects, a subservient life, will be miserable. If, [however], the

---

[113] This is a popular aphorism, appearing in many devotional songs and even as the title of a self-development "bestseller" by Umesh Kumarawat: *man ke hāre hār hai, man ke jīte jīt*।

things of this world become subservient to your mind, then your mind becomes victorious and like a conqueror, you will always be blissful. Hence, become a conqueror, and become independent for the fulfillment of life is found only in independence.

Therefore protect yourself from excessive worldly objects, and more than that, protect yourself from constantly thinking about worldly objects.

## *Teaching #50*

**Wherever the mind is inclined to go, it sets out on that path by itself**

ॐ

All things depend solely on the mind. As the mind desires, so a man acts. Action or inaction, everything depends totally on the mind. If the mind has decided on action, whether enjoined or not prescribed (*vihita-āvihita*), it will find a way to carry it out. If the mind is pure, it will be inclined towards pure actions, and to the same extent those actions will be powerful and long-lasting (*sthāyī).* Similarly, if the mind is dirty and impure, it will be inclined to the impure, and its actions will be very weak and of but fleeting importance.

For all kinds of progress, both in this world and the next, keep the mind pure, and it is essential to increase the purity of the mind to remain pure. Therefore you must keep the company of good people while forgoing the company of the bad. Always study the scriptures; take care to maintain a pure diet; perform Bhagavān's *bhajan* and worship, as well as repetition of *mantras*; practice truth and non-injury (*ahimsā*), and the other precepts of good conduct; you must always keep yourself within proper bounds.

## *Teaching #51*

### Attachment is the root of all miseries

ॐ

Attachment (*rāga*) is absent in the enlightened person, and attachment remains within the ignorant person. An enlightened person's activities will be free from attachment, and will unfold according to currently manifesting (*prārabdha*) *karma*; an ignorant person's activities also will unfold according to currently manifesting (*prārabdha) karma*, but throughout this there will remain attachment, because attachment is understood to be the very mark of the unenlightened. Attachment alone binds the individual to the shackles of birth and death. When attachment no longer remains, an individual becomes liberated. It's like this,

[Sanskrit:] *vītarāga janmādarśanāt* ।[114]

This is a saying from the *Roga Śāstra*—it means, when attachment is destroyed, then there is no rebirth. Hence try to destroy this great binder and root of all miseries called attachment. When attachment towards *saṃsāra* occurs, then one will turn towards Paramātmā.

---

[114] Literally, "without attachment, rebirth is no longer seen."

# *Teaching #52*

**Don't let fear of obstacles deter you from your path; there is no fear of falling, for Bhagavān will protect you**

ॐ

After coming to know Bhagavān, there is nothing else worth knowing. Once you have enjoyed the taste of God-realization (*Bhagavatattva)*, then one's disposition cannot be entangled in any other object. How can a king crave becoming the landlord of a couple of villages? How can one who is immersed in the ocean of bliss desire for transient pleasures, the pleasures born of worldly objects? People say, "This so and so *mahātma* had fallen, that so and so Maharishi had fallen." But how do you recognize the small and great? *Mahātmās* have never fallen nor can they ever fall. To fall is possible only for aspirants who have yet to attain. But he to whom Bhagavān has appeared can never have such a disposition that he covets the pleasures born of worldly contacts. Being a *mahātma* or an enlightened person is in one's disposition. No one can know what state another person is in — that is self-experiential (sv*asaṁvedya*).

Bhagavān has said that "my three-strand *māyā* is difficult to escape,"[115] meaning crossing it [to the other shore] is quite difficult. But he who comes to me for shelter will cross this difficult *māyā* of mine:

[Sanskrit:] *Daivī hyeṣā guṇamayī mama māyā duratyayā*।

*Mām eva ye prapadyante māyām etāṃ taranti te* ॥[116]

---

[115]By three-strand *māyā* he refers to *prakṛti*, or material nature, which is composed of the three *guṇas* or qualities: *sattva*, *rajas*, and *tamas*.

Therefore, don't let fear of obstacles deter you from your path. Bhagavān will protect you in every way, and will bring you close to him. There is no need to fear a fall, just keep going on the path.

## *Teaching #53*

### To prevent inclination for the bad and to apply oneself to the good: this is the primary human goal (*puruṣārtha*)

ॐ

The primary human goal is to inhibit inclination toward bad action, and increase inclination to good action. If any bad impulses arise, then set your mind to chanting, singing spiritual songs, reading spiritual books, reciting stories about the divine, and so on. This is the teaching of the *Upaniṣads*.

[Sanskrit:] *śubhāśubhābhyāṃ mārgābhyāṃ vahanti vāsanā sarita*।
*pauruṣeṇa prayatnena yojanīyā śubho pathi*।। *Muktika Upaniṣad 2.2.5*

The river of impulses (*vāsāna*) flows in two streams: the good and the bad. One should channel it only toward the good path (*śubha mārga*). Whenever a bad impulse arises, the ideal human goal is to turn the mind in the other direction and strive not to act on it. "I will wait to take action on this thought, tomorrow I'll do it" — thinking this way, let some time pass, and then this impulse will certainly be calmed. If a good impulse should arise in your mind,

---

[116] *Bhagavad Gītā* 7.14: "This divine *māyā* of mine consisting of the *guṇas* is indeed very difficult to overcome; those who have surrendered to me can certainly overcome this *māyā*."

then be ready to act on it immediately. If possible, try to start that work without delay.

When bad impulses arise in the mind, then try to stop them and somehow refrain from them, and should a good impulse arise, then try to act on it as quickly as possible: this is the human goal (*puruṣārtha*).

## *Teaching #54*

**When one turns away from Paramātmā, all types of distress swarm around**

ॐ

In whatever land you live, one can remain happy and peaceful only by following its laws and regulations. If you disobey the orders of the king, then you will surely be punished. The lord of the whole universe is the universal ruler Paramātmā. If you act against his wishes, you will inevitably have to accept his punishment. These days people have turned away from Paramātmā, because of which unrest, dissatisfaction, and sorrow are on the rise daily.

The divine law (*īsvarīya niyam*) is equally beneficial for everyone. To whatever extent a person follows the law well, to that very extent he will experience happiness and peace. The Vedas and *śāstras* themselves are the teachings of Paramātmā that benefit everyone. By following them, all manner of improvements are possible. By implementing the spiritual laws mentioned in the *Vedas* and *śāstras*, man can increase his power, capability, knowledge, and bliss limitlessly.

When you are able to sell diamonds, then why blacken your hands by touting coal? When by worshiping Paramātmā according to rule you can obtain endless bliss, then why struggle day and night to collect ephemeral sensory pleasures? Act with a little power of discrimination; don't just drift along with the times with your eyes shut. Day and night will pass as they will, but if you misuse even one moment, it is a matter of your own improvement. Therefore, immersing yourself in Paramātmā, act according to your own *dharma* — this is the path of complete advancement.

## *Teaching #55*

### The human goal (*puruṣārtha*) is stronger than currently manifesting (*prārabdha*) *karma*

ॐ

Your past goals are appearing before you today as your present currently manifesting (*prārabdha) karma*. Stale past drives become fresh, currently manifesting (*prārabdha) karma*. If you make something today, then it will be stale by tomorrow. Whatever thing you make today, will arise again before you tomorrow; whatever you have made before, that will come before you today, and what you make today, will come again in the future. The happiness and sorrow that comes in your life today are the fruit of your past good and bad *karma*. Now act so that you do not create the groundwork for future sorrow. It is certain that whatever actions you perform, you will have to consume their fruit. If you perform approved activities, good acts, then their fruit will bear happiness, and if you perform inappropriate acts, then they will appear before you as sorrow.

If you want to make your future currently manifesting (*prārabdha) karma* good, then at this time, with the help of your own *puruṣārtha*, do superior deeds. Ascertain what constitutes superior deeds for someone in accord with the view of the *śāstras*. If you engage in right action according to your proper position (*adhikāra*), then you will be more peaceful and happy in the present and superior commenced *karma* will be the future result.

Whatever good or bad situations are confronting you right now, these are surely your currently manifesting (*prārabdha) karma* that stand waiting to be experienced. But it is not true that whatever comes before you must be experienced. Even currently manifesting (*prārabdha) karma* must be accompanied properly by discrimination. If wine and meat are placed in front of you, then understanding this as the fruit of past evil *karma*, through discrimination you should reject them: do not accept them, and destroy their evil results by chanting and asceticism.

It is the established teaching that *japato' nāstipātakam* ।[117]

"By chanting, sins will be destroyed." Therefore, experience your currently manifesting (*prārabdha) karma* appropriately and destroy the inappropriate through chanting and asceticism. By thus performing your daily activities with discrimination, you will make progress, because if you are not careful in your daily activities, then you will wallow in the mud like a dog or a pig.

---

[117] Verse 5 of the popular *108 Names of Viṣṇu Stotra.*

## *Teaching #56*

### There are many renouncers and benefactors; try instead to become very attached and miserly

ॐ

The greatest of all renouncers is considered to be he who renounces the greatest thing possible. In this universe, the greatest thing is Paramātmā. They who renounce Paramātmā and are turned away from Bhagavān are the greatest renouncers. He who acts on behalf of others can be said to be generous, and he who acts only for himself is a miser. He who takes all that he has earned and deposits it in a bank under his own name can be called miserly.

A truly attached person is one whose mind never leaves the objects of attachment. It is the mark of an attached person that wherever he places his mind, it doesn't rise from there. Such attachment is found in Paramātmā, who is the ultimate object of attraction. Whosever has attached his mind to Bhagavān, and cannot divert it from him — he is the truly attached person; strive to become such an attached person. There is no need to renounce *saṃsāra*; increase your attachment to Paramātmā, and become a truly attached person.

Those people who are always involved in the affairs of *saṃsāra* are benevolent in reality, because whatever they do will be useful for others, and nothing will continue on with them. And those who have acquired a lot of merit by charity, virtue, chanting, austerities, etc., can in reality be said to be miserly. Because here, all the fruits of all their actions are being bundled into a parcel addressed to themselves. In the future, they alone will receive it — and nobody else. In this way meritorious people in reality can be said to be miserly. Becoming miserly like this in this world, you will receive great fame in this life, and in the next world, too, you will gain the best path; this is the established teaching (*siddhānta*) of the *śāstras*.

## *Teaching #57*

### Grab onto the one Bhagavān steadfastly, then you will not have to flatter the many

ॐ

Make your main chosen deity the all-capable Bhagavān, whose very form is bliss, and maintain a stance of undividedness toward him, and then you will lack for nothing. If you grab on to that One steadfastly, you will be freed from flattering the many, otherwise you will go from door to door like a stray dog wagging its tail, and your precious life will be used up seeking food and clothing. The stray dog may get bread here and there, but must endure blows everywhere. He who has not accepted a chosen deity will at all times be like an orphan, despite however much money and comforts he has found.

To be devoted undividedly to a chosen deity means that during the time of worshipping the chosen one, if any worldly affairs come up, then you ignore them and remain undisturbed from your worship. In your life, understand the greater goal as primary and worldly activities as secondary. Have faith in the pledge of Bhagavān, then you can keep your head high both in *saṃsāra* and the next world.

[Sanskrit:] *ananyāścintayanto māṁ ye janāḥ paryupāsate*।

*teṣāṁ nityābhiyuktānāṁ yogakṣemaṁ vahāmyaham* || [118]

This means, "Whoever thinks of me with an undivided attitude, for him I take care of his yoga [obtaining those things which are not yet obtained] and protection [protecting those things which are already obtained]." This is the pledge of Bhagavān. Having faith in this, you will always be happy.

## *Teaching #58*

### ***Saṃsāra*** **will go on like it always has;**

### **while you are here, attend to your own work**

ॐ

Exceedingly great warriors and powerful conquerors have come, but all eventually become the chewed up morsels of Time (*Kāla*) — today there is no trace of them. But this *saṃsāra* goes on precisely the same like a stream. Intelligence is such that it is limited to the extent that it enables only your own work. By putting your life's effort into attaining Paramātmā who is existence, knowledge, and bliss, you should try to fulfill yourself in every way possible. Don't get entangled in this vicious cycle of *saṃsāra*, because it will go on like it always has; it is useless to increase the mirage. Don't light your own *Holī* fire by your own hands.[119]

---

[118] *Bhagavad Gītā* 9.22.

[119] The fire celebrated in the festival of *Holī* is believed to be a funeral pyre, since it was the means of destroying the demoness Holikā.

Is it wise to leave your own house unclean while trying to clean the houses of your neighbors? First do your own work, and then you can help do others' work. First complete that work for which you have come into this world. If you do not take care of yourself first, but instead foolishly waste your time trying to take care of others, you will regret it at the end. Wisdom consists in making the best of both this and the next world. This is possible only if you consider your primary task in life to be the ultimate goal. Make the ultimate goal primary and make all other good acts of *saṃsāra* secondary. Carry out praise, worship, meditation, and adoration regularly and consider them to be your primary task. Draw out some time from those activities and carry out some good acts of *saṃsāra*, otherwise you will be cheated.

## *Teaching #59*

**Human birth is rare, make it useful**

Whatever has happened has happened, but now proceed carefully

Don't sell a diamond for the price of spinach

ॐ

After experiencing 8,400,000 births, we have obtained this rare human body; don't waste it. Each and every moment of life is very valuable. And if you don't understand its value? Then you will have nothing else to do but weep, and you will have nothing in your hands in the end.

You are a human being, therefore you have the power to discriminate what is good and what is bad, and you can accomplish the greatest human goals. Don't think of yourself as weak or fallen. Whatever has happened in the past, understand that it was done unknowingly. But now be careful, begin doing the type of acts appropriate for a human being. Discern for yourself what is good and what is bad. Adopt the good and reject the bad.

As a human being, if you don't know Paramātmā, then understand that you have sold a diamond for the price of spinach. One does not worship Paramātmā for the sake of Paramātmā. One worships Paramātmā to remove one's own sorrow, lack of peace, ignorance, and lack of power. Paramātmā is all knowing, omnipotent, and full of limitless bliss. Through worship, one can grasp on to his unending power. The fulfillment of this superb act is the real purpose of human life. If there is no effort made toward this, then understand that you have cheated yourself.

## *Teaching #60*

**If you want power (*śakti*), attach yourself to the source of power.**

**It is foolish to imagine happiness in *saṃsāra*, the very ocean of sorrow**

ॐ

Attach yourself to Paramātmā, who is the source of unending power, then your inner organ's (*antah kanaṇa*) poverty will cease. *Saṃsāra* is not something to be known, it is something to be forgotten. The more you try to understand this ocean of sorrows, the more you will plunge into far greater sorrow. To hope that by comprehending *saṃsāra* you will attain happiness and peace is like wanting to find light by searching in darkness.

*Saṃsāra* is the ocean of sorrow. It is impossible to become happy with the help of this ocean of sorrow. To love *saṃsāra* is to sow the seeds of sorrow.

[Sanskrit:] "*yatra snehī tatra duḥkhasya bhājanam*/[120]

Don't love this world, you should just keep doing only your worldly duties.

Perform your worldly activities in *saṃsāra*, like you are conducting your daily activities with an enemy. When an enemy comes to your door, welcome him more graciously than a friend, because a friend will not be concerned about formalities, but an enemy will take great notice of even the smallest slight. Therefore, an enemy should be welcomed with complete formalities. Thus, in *saṃsāra* observe all formalities in good fashion, but inwardly understand that this is an enemy. This does not mean you should start feeling friendly toward this world. If *saṃsāra* becomes desireable in your mind, then you will be cheated. Don't try to know too much of this.

## *Teaching #61*

**Those for whom you are straining and struggling will reject you**

ॐ

You should accept as certain that we must by necessity leave *saṃsāra*, and abandon everything; nothing can accompany us, that is certain. When nothing can accompany you when you go, then for the time you must remain here, abide without worrying. Do not experience restlessness from worthless worries.

---

[120] In other words, "Wherever there is desire, there is experience of sorrow."

We should certainly live for the sake of our own livelihood, because by necessity we must bear our currently manifesting (*prarabdha*) *karma* — it will find us by itself — so there is no need to worry about that. And if you are worried about others, then just ask yourself and just watch: those for whom you are straining and struggling will eventually reject you.

In *saṃsāra*, everybody will be friendly to the fortunate. "Everyone will act as the wife's brother to the prosperous, but no one will act as the sister's husband to the spoiled."[121] Maharishi Vālmīki's earlier name was Mārkaṇḍeya. He used to raid travelers to feed and clothe his family. Once a group of rishis came his way. Mārkaṇḍeya raided them. The rishis told him, "We will not run away, but ask your family this, 'Are you ready to share the demerit acquired through raiding others or not? Or do you just want the wealth?'" Mārkaṇḍeya went and asked his relatives. They all said, "We will not take the demerit—we just want the wealth. If you are earning all this money by committing sins, then only you should bear the demerit." Having received this response from his family members, Mārkaṇḍeya understood and he decided, "Whatever mistakes that I have committed have already been done, and now they must be corrected. I have just a little more time in this life, so it should not be wasted."

At that time Mārkaṇḍeya began uttering " Rāma, Rāma," according to the instructions of the rishis,[122] and having sat down on a seat, he became so deeply engrossed in the *bhajan* of Bhagavān that ants made a big hill—a

---

[121] This saying plays on extended family dynamics.

[122] In many versions, the man who would become the greatest devotee of the lord Rāma was actually instructed to chant the *mantra*, *mārā* — "kill" — but because he chanted it over and over, the sound was rendered auspicious into the name of God: *rāmārāmāmā*.

*valmīkaḥ*—around him. Later, he came out of the anthill, so his name became Vālmīki "*valmīkodyavaḥ*: *vālmīkaḥ*."[123]

The gist of this story is that in *saṃsāra*, if you strain and struggle for others by committing offenses, then this world and the next will both be spoiled. Hence it is wise to perform your worldly activities honestly and spend your time peacefully doing the *bhajan* of Bhagavān.

## *Teaching #62*

### Why do we abuse and throw colored powder on Holī?

ॐ

Today is the time of Holī. You should understand what this is all about. Prahalāda's aunt, who was also Hiraṇyakaśipu's sister, was named Dūṅḍā (she was also called Holikā). She had done *tapas* and had received a boon that she could safely sit in fire, and drawing someone into her lap, that person would be burnt up. Hiraṇyakaśipu had become exhausted from attacking Prahalāda, and he was unable to trouble him at all — he had thrown Prahalāda down from mountaintops and Prahalāda merely laughed; dunked him under water, and Prahalāda emerged smiling; threw him into fire, but he was unburned. In this way, when Hiraṇyakaśipu had done all this yet failed, and Prahalāda would not abandon worshipping Bhagavān, then Dūṇḍa said, "Bring him, and I will burn him to ashes." Dūṇḍa placed Prahalāda onto her lap and sat down. A fire began

---

[123] He is simply giving the derivation of the name from the Sanskrit term for anthill (*valmīkaḥ*).

burning in all four directions. But the power of Prahalāda's devotion was such that instead Dūṇḍa burned up and Prahalāda came out of the fire smiling.

On the occasion of Holī, people hurl abuses and use obscene words, and all of these insults are for Dūṅḍā. These dirty words are like hymns to demons, because demonic powers are pleased with words of this kind. By this, the place of Dūṇḍa is kept alive in the world, and it also serves to remind us that someone as powerful as Dūṇḍa, who had the elements such as fire under her control, nevertheless, if even such a person as she who rises up in opposition to a devotee of Bhagavān, then can have their very same powers turn against them, while protecting the devotee. This is the secret of hurling abuses on the holiday of Holī.

Whatever colors and powders are used on the day of Holī symbolize happiness. The happiness of people meeting each other expresses their joy that on this day, the demonic powers that tried to destroy the great devotee of Bhagavān Prahalāda was herself burned to ashes. "This is the celebration of the annihilation of that demoness who was torturing the devotee Prahalāda." This is the greatness of Holī.

## *Teaching #63*

**How was the son of the great demon Hiraṇyakaśipu born a great devotee?**

ॐ

Once upon a time, after having been defeated in a war with the gods, the demon Hiraṇyakaśipu went to the forest to perform *tapas* with the goal of accumulating greater power. At that time, his wife was pregnant. Indra thought that Hiraṇyakaśipu's son might become more powerful than his father, and he would create even greater trouble for the gods, so it would be good to kill the child immediately at its birth. With this objective in mind, Indra carried off the pregnant wife of Hiraṇyakaśipu. Along the road, she was lamenting, and they happened to run into the sage Nārada ji. He asked Indra, "Where are you taking this defenseless lady? And for what purpose?" Indra replied, "This is the wife of Hiraṇyakaśipu, and she is pregnant; when I destroy the child who will be born to her, I will be quickly removing a future trouble for the gods, so I am taking her to my world." Nārada said, "From her womb, a great devotee of Bhagavān will be born, and he will be unconquerable, so release her." Having heard Nārada's words, Indra released her and departed. Nārada then took her to his ashram, where he narrated devotional stories of Bhagavān constantly.

A pregnant woman's environment, including the things she hears and sees, has a great effect on the child in her womb. When this child, whose name was Prahalāda, started going to school, he told his classmates about wisdom and meditation as well as stories of Bhagavān. The other children asked, "You study with us, yet these things are not taught here, and you live in the company of demons (*daityas*), so you never get the opportunity to receive this kind of education, so how have you come to learn the wonderful things that you are telling us people about?"

Prahalāda told them about the things he heard while he was in the womb. "My mother went to Nārada's ashram, and Maharishi Nārada had told her constantly stories of Bhagavān, so I had heard all these in my mother's womb. After returning from the ashram, my mother was in the environment of demons (*daityas*), so my mother completely forgot all those things, but I remembered everything. That is what I am telling you all."

The son of Hiraṇyakaśipu, King of the Daityas, had heard the conversation of *satsaṅga* while he was still in the womb, and was born the king of devotees. Even today, if pregnant women live in a righteous and devotional atmosphere, and hear excellent righteous things, then even today they can give birth to a Dhruva or Prahalāda. But nowadays they get no break from the cinema and reading dirty books. This leads to giving birth to misbehaving and characterless children who cause their parents to weep from their birth. It is the rituals (*samskāra*) of a pregnant woman that affect the rituals of a child in the womb, and can thus instill faith. To give birth to a child like an animal is one thing, but if you want superior intelligent and well-behaved children, then keep a woman in a pure atmosphere during pregnancy. After the ritual of *garbhadhāna* according to the scriptural rules, keep a woman from *rajasic* or *tamasic* things. From the expectant mother's superior emotional well-being, the child in the womb will be endowed with superior qualities.

Prahalāda was sure that Bhagavān is everywhere. He knew that Paramātmā was everywhere. Wherever he looked, he saw his chosen deity. Prahalāda had indisputable certainty that Paramātmā was everywhere.[124] He saw his Rām in everything: water, soil, and fire. This was the reason that water, fire, and all the other elements could not harm him — such was the faith of a five-year-old in Bharata.[125] If the Indian people come back to their established truths, then no power in all the three worlds can trouble them. But they have forgotten the things of their own house and have become completely impoverished. When the almighty Paramātman again favors them, then all the powers of material nature will favor them as well. Whatever means were used to try to trouble Prahalāda became favorable to him. When they had thrown him into fire, then he said with a smile,

---

[124] Here Guru Dev emphasizes Phahalāda knew that all three—Bhagavān, *Paramātman, iṣṭa devatā* — were everywhere.

[125] He who is a descendent of Bharat.

[Sanskrit:] *rāmanāmajapatāṁ kuto bhayaṁ*

*sarvatāpaśamanaikabheṣajam* |

*paśya tāta mamagānnasannidhau*

*pāvako 'pi salilāyate 'dhunā* ||

This means, "Where is the fear of the person who chants the name of Rām? This (name of Rām) is the medicine that removes all types of sorrow. O Father! See how now the fire near my body acts like water," meaning that it was cooling.

The point is so long as we confine our chosen deity in one small tin box of limited space, then we will suffer accordingly, and we must struggle along without recourse like a cripple. If you begin to see your chosen deity as pervading everywhere, then whatever will come close will become your chosen one, and appear as your friend. This is an established doctrine (*siddhānta*), for the one whose faith is well-formed, then whatever approaches him will become as the person himself.

Patañjali, the author of the *Yoga Śāstra*, has written:

[Sanskrit:] *ahiṁsāpratiṣṭhāyāṁ tatsannidhau vairatyāgaḥ* ||[126]

If one has strong faith in nonviolence, then the lion, tiger, and all harmful animals, for instance, will abandon their self-dispositions, and become nonviolent. But our faith should be very strong, our trust in Paramātmā should be firm. It does not mean one should follow anybody that one sees with a copper pot in his hand.[127] The washerman's dog belongs neither to a home nor the

---

[126] *Yoga Sūtra* 2.35, "In the presence of one firmly grounded in non-violence, they abandon their hostility."

[127] The metal pot is one of the signs of an ascetic's vows and thus a social marker.

riverbank."[128] We should act thoughtfully, it isn't good to waste everything for the sake of filling our bellies. All types of animals — even insects and birds — live to care for their bellies. If, as a human being, you live to care for your belly, then what is the point of the human birth? Indians (*Bhāratīyas*) never place importance to their bellies. Here first preference is always given for the spirituality.

Maharishis of old who lived on nothing but fruits and water had the capacity to make even world-ruling kings obey their commands. In those days there were devotees who used to eat *halva-puris* and *rabadi-mulai*,[129] but they knew that if they ate *halva-puri* and such things then their intellect would become clouded and would make them fall. If the intellects of individuals such as Bhīṣma[130] can become clouded due to impure grain, then what could happen to the people of today? So to keep the intellect pure, one should always remain aware of the purity of one's food, and with the help of Bhagavān, one should try to sustain oneself with a pure (*sattvik*) lifestyle.

---

[128] In other words, the working dog of a *dhobi* or washerman neither stays in the house nor is it a stray.

[129] Rich, creamy dishes reserved for special persons and occasions.

[130] A great hero of the *Mahābhārata*.

# Teaching #64

**Become humble[131] to gain the blessings of the all-merciful**

ॐ

Bhagavān is supremely merciful. He shows mercy to the humble. Man should try to please Bhagavān with his humility, or by his worshiping; also, by carrying out one's own enjoined duties, one may offer the fruits of actions in worship of Bhagavān. If one cannot carry out such *karma* and worship, then at least one should become humble. Who is humble? Whoever has no support in *saṃsāra* is humble. Bhagavān is wholly the support of the unsupported. This is his great compassion. The person whose attachments to the world are totally gone — support of a wife, children, money, friends, etc. — such a supportless humble one will be supported by Paramātmā, who is ever the world-supporter, friend of the poor, destitute, and weak.

Draupadī, during her disrobing,[132] became humble: nobody was there to protect her. Such was her miserable condition that when she called on Bhagavān, then Bhagavān, friend of the destitute, protected her.

All must reap the fruits of their past actions, but the humble gain a special right, such that they don't have to suffer the results of past *karma*. Hence, if you cannot carry out any other practice, then at least become humble.

---

[131] The term *dīn* can be used both as an adjective and a noun. Its meanings can be rendered humble, destitute, or poverty-stricken, or a person characterized by such qualities.

[132] In one of the greatest scenes of the *Mahābhārata*, Draupadī is lost to her husbands' cousin Duryodhana when wagered in a crooked dice match, and she is forced to endure disrobing in the presence of all the great generals in the assembly. Calling on lord Kṛṣṇa to preserve her honor, Draupadī's sari is magically lengthened by him, saving her from public nudity and further dishonor.

When man becomes humble, then the world will appear to him like a magician's money. There may appear to be a heap of millions of rupees, but when it is announced, "This is just a magician's cache" then even the most miserly, greedy person will not bother looking at it. Similarly, when one becomes humble, he will not have any attachment to anything whatsoever in this world. When a man calls on Bhagavān without any attachment to *saṃsāra* in a state of humility, then he will be worthy of the friend of the destitute Bhagavān's compassion. The delay is in becoming humble: the compassionate one is ever ready to support you.

Due to lack of *satsaṅga*, people are not able to make use of the compassionate self-nature of Bhagavān. Furthermore, whatever little people may gain from *satsaṅga*, doesn't stay in their mind and heart (*antaḥ karaṇa)*. The reason is lack of purity in food.

Just as looking at food will not appease one's hunger, listening to the glory of the name of Bhagavān by itself will not give happiness and peace. Nowadays it has become very popular to chant the *Bhagavad Gītā*. Chanting itself is definitely meritorious, but full happiness and peace are impossible to obtain through its recitation alone. If just one verse of the *Gītā* is understood, or one fourth of a single verse, then auspicious results are possible.

# *Teaching #65*

**Always do your own enjoined duties and remember Bhagavān**

ॐ

The individual should remember Bhagavān for his own benefit, not for Bhagavān's. Bhagavān never becomes pleased with anybody, nor angry. The individual remembers [him] only for his own welfare.

There are many methods of remembering Bhagavān. One has to learn this from his Guru according to one's own convenience.

Kabir was a great devotee of Rāma. He constantly sang the name of Bhagavān Rāma. Throughout his daily activities, even while carrying out his weaving, he chanted, Rām, Rām, Rām. By continuously taking the name of Bhagavān like this, he developed firm faith and he achieved perfection in the name.[133] There is an interesting incident which reveals exactly what this perfection in the name is.

Once a leper who thought that his disease was incurable came to Kabir's house. People go to *mahātmās* only after they have exhausted all other means, like Ayurvedic masters and doctors. At that time Kabir was not in his house, and this leper explained his situation to Kabir's wife. She felt compassionate and told the patient to chant the name of Rām three times and he would become well. Then the leper explained that he had taken the name of Rām thousands of times, but nothing had happened. The lady insisted, "Do as I say." When he had taken

---

[133] *Nāma siddha*, mastery of the name, is a specific kind of spiritual achievement that involves mastery of the name of god as one's *mantra*. The tradition of *nāma siddha* can be traced from the Nāths and Siddha Yoga traditions through the modern day Sikhs, who hold Kabir to be one of their most dear saints and illustrative masters of the Name.

the name of Rām three times, his body became totally cured. He became extremely happy and left. Along the way, he praised the glories of Kabir. Kabir was coming along that same way. He heard this person saying that if anyone has any problem, he should go to Kabir Sahab's house. Kabir greeted this gentleman and said, "I am Kabir. From now on, if you tell anybody about your being cured, you will have problems, and you will never be well again."

After saying this, Kabir returned to the house and assumed a sad appearance. Any husband-loving woman who is devoted to her husband can bear anything, but she cannot bear her husband's sadness. This is the sign of *pativratyā*.[134] She asked Kabir about his sadness, and Kabir said, "The thing is this, you have made Bhagavān's name very cheap. By taking Bhagavān's name just once, he could have gotten a divine body, so why did you make him utter it thrice? It's possible that your asking him to repeat it thrice is because you did not have sufficient faith in just one time."

The point is that Bhagavān's name has more inherent power to destroy the effects of more sins than anybody could ever commit. There is such great power to burn in fire, that nobody can ever accumulate sufficient wood [to exhaust it].

[Sanskrit:] *harir harati pāpāni duṣṭacittairapismṛtaḥ* |[135]

---

[134] *Pativratyā* is the auspicious state of a woman who has made a vow (*vrata*) to be supportive and true to her husband (*pati*), making him her end of life and even treating him as her chosen deity.

[135] Literally, "Even remembering Hari with an evil mind destroys sin." This is the first portion of a famous verse attributed to various sources, including the *Bṛhat Nāradiya Purāṇa* 1.10.100, but more popularly it is known as the first verse in the *Hari Aṣṭaka*, or "Eight Verses to Hari" many Vaiṣṇava devotees learn by heart. The second half of the

"When one remembers [him] even with an evil mind, Bhagavān will destroy one's sins." Hence continuing good actions, carrying out all your own enjoined duties, and always remembering Bhagavān, let all your past sins be destroyed. But one should not continue committing sins while taking the name of Bhagavān. After all, what profit is there if one continuously withdraws whatever one deposits in the bank?

## *Teaching #66*

### Contemplation on Bhagavān and a pure diet

ॐ

Until we experience something, our faith in it cannot be firm; thoughts of *saṃsāra* will always remain. Hence thinking of Paramātmā must be difficult. Bhagavān has said,

[Sanskrit:] *maccittā madgata prāṇaḥ bodhayantaḥ parasparam* ।

*kathayantaśca māṁ nityaṃ tuṣyanti ca ramanti ca* ।।[136]

The sense of this is to "Attach your thoughts to me," not thoughts of *saṃsāra*, but rather think of Paramātmā. The point is that Bhagavān at no time and in no situation leaves—he never leaves one's thoughts. The main cause of

---

verse is: *anicchayāpi saṁspruṣṭo dahatyevahi pāvaka* ।।, meaning "Just as fire, on contacting an object, automatically burns it."

[136] The text is corrupt, but Guru Dev is clearly quoting *Bhagavad Gītā* 10.9, so I have provided the correct Sanskrit. The verse means: "The thoughts of my pure devotees dwell in me, their lives are fully devoted to my service, and they derive great satisfaction and bliss from always enlightening one another and conversing about me."

many worries is impurity in our diet. With regard to the purity of food, Dhanārjana has said,

[Sanskrit:] *akṛtvā parasantāpaṃ, āgatvā khalamandiram* |

*anullaṅghya satām vartmaṃ yadalpamapi tad bahu* ||

This means, not harming others, not associating with bad persons, not plunging the *ātman* in entanglements, and whatever small amount we earn will be plenty. If you make trouble for others while earning your money, that wealth will remain behind, but the harm that you have given to the person will carry along with your subtle body. Therefore, don't act such that you carry along a baggage of sin with you.

The meaning of *āgatvā khalamandiram* is this — if you associate with base people, your intellect (*buddhi*) gets spoiled, and once your intellect is spoiled, a fall is certain.

[The phrase] *buddhināśāt praṇasyati* — Direct association with base objects is much more precipitous. So going to the home of the wicked for the purpose of making money is forbidden.

The meaning of *anullaṅghya satām vartmaṃ* is this—that path which is in accord with the Vedas and *śāstras* given by good people should never be violated.

If a situation arises in your daily dealings where you have to come into contact with a base person, then you should approach him just like you go to the toilet — do the job and leave. Nobody lingers in the toilet for long. If you discipline your intellect in this way, then there is no doubt of harm through association with the low. A pure mind goes near Paramātmā, and the impure mind wanders through various types of emotional states. Therefore, through pure food, we should keep trying especially to purify the mind: it is necessary to give much more attention to cleaning grains. If you maintain proper diet, you will think of Bhagavān, so it is essential the mind be pure. With a pure mind, even in this world you will experience happiness and peace, and you will obtain the best path in the next world as well.

## *Teaching #67*

### Avoid further births as a human

ॐ

Now that you have obtained a human body, you should not hold open the possibility that you will come back again to the womb. There is no point to human life if you return again and again to the womb, and the purpose of human birth has not been served.

Individual *jīvas* are infinite in number, but according to the *Purāṇas* there are 8,400,000 different species. The *jīva* evolves through this 8,400,000 species, and then attains a human body.

Envision a big circular compound composed of 8,400,000 cells. A blind man has been living in one block and wants to come out. Thinking that there must be a door somewhere, he guides himself along the wall, going from one cell to another. Just as he reaches the gate, he removes his hand from the wall to scratch an itch, and he misses the gate by walking further.

The secret behind this story is that the blind person is the *jīva* and the cells are the 8,400,000 species. The human species is the way to emerge from this cycle. When *jīva* comes to the gate, that is the human species, he starts enjoying wealth, women, children, etc., which is the itching. Like the blind man, he misses the purpose of the human species by wasting time scratching his itch.

*Śāstras* says again and again that a human birth is very rare. This does not mean that when we get this rare human body we should pursue wealth, children, and the enjoyment of maximum worldly pleasure. Then there would be no point in the human birth being rare. Humanity is the *karma* species and other animals (like insects and birds) are the enjoyment (*bhoga*) species. In the *bhoga* species, there is no accounting for actions. But whatever action *jīva* undertakes with the help of a human body will be taken into account and there will be a result of every action. Therefore the human species is very difficult to attain. After transmigrating through 8,400,000 *bhoga* species we get this human body. Having gained this human body, we can perform such actions as will help to escape the cycle of birth and death so that the wandering of *jīva* will come to an end and there will be no further chance to suffer in mother's womb.

*Śāstra* says that if a human worships the gods, he goes to the world of the gods, and if he worships ghosts, then he goes to the world of the ghosts.

[Sanskrit:] *bhūtāni yānti bhūtejyā* ।[137]

He who worships ghosts (*bhūtejyā)* earns the birth (*yoni*) of a ghost, and [who worships the] gods earns the birth of a god.

By doing *japa* and *tapa* (austerities), one attains godhood (*devattā*). But the aim of a human being should not be to gain godhood, because even the most powerful among the gods, even the king of all the gods, displayed a lack of discrimination and desire for worldly enjoyment. And when he could not fulfill all his desires in heaven, then he came to the world of death and troubled Ahilyā.

---

[137] *Bhagavad Gītā* 9.25c: "worshippers of the departed (*bhūtāni*, ghosts) go to the departed."

When this is the story of the king of the gods, then what will be the condition of his subjects? Therefore, we should prostrate [worship] them from the distance.

The second thing is this, the state of *jīva* in heaven also has its time limitation.

[Sanskrit:] *kṣiṇe puṇye martyalokaṁ viśanti Bhagavad Gītā* 9.21

After exhausting all its merit, the *jīva* has to come back to the world of death *(martyalokaṁ).* But even there all do not share an equal degree of happiness. Each revels in luxury according to the merit he has accumulated. Then the subjects in heaven are jealous, seeing that another is enjoying more than they are. In heaven, too, we find jealousy, mercy, and hatred, which cause unhappiness. We should not desire to go to such a heaven at all.

Even the gods (*devas*) also desire to have a human body, because the human species is like molten gold. Ornaments are not made of pure gold. With a good goldsmith, one can turn gold into valuable ornaments. Such an ornament can raise the value of the gold to the highest level. Gods in heaven are more like such ornaments than they are like pure gold. Once an ornament is made, the value of that gold is fixed. The human species is like pure gold. If he finds the perfect goldsmith, he can attain infinite bliss, experience Parabrahma directly, or he can become Paramātmā itself, and if this happens, birth as a human being is fulfilled.

## *Teaching #68*

### The sign of the devotee is experiencing Bhagavān everywhere

ॐ

All devotees who are enraptured with the divine are Vaiṣṇava devotees. Anyone involved day and night in stealing, cheating, and other evil activity cannot be a Vaiṣṇava just by calling himself a devotee of Viṣṇu, thus Vaiṣṇava.

Śiva, Gaṇeśa, Sūrya, Śakti,[138] and so on, are all limbs of Bhagavān. A devotee of Śiva may say, My Śiva is Bhagavān, and a devotee of Sūrya may say, "Sūrya is Bhagavān," so it is like not knowing the true form of an entire elephant. Some blind people caught hold of the trunk and said, "This elephant is like a mortar pestle." One caught hold of its leg and said, "An elephant is like a pillar." Another caught hold of its ear and said, "An elephant is like a fan." The point is, "The blind began to quarrel on seeing the elephant,"—the one who knows the complete, true form of an elephant won't describe an elephant to be like a fan or as a pestle.

In the same way, one who has truly understood Bhagavān will never say that Śiva is the true form of Bhagavān, or Gaṇeśa is the true form of Bhagavān, or Lord Viṣṇu in his four-armed form is the true form of Bhagavān. One who is acquainted with the divine truth will say this—in all these various forms, one Paramātmā is manifest, or these five deities have the form of various limbs of

---

[138] Śiva is the great ascetic deity, famous as the destroyer of the universe; Gaṇeśa is the popular elephant-headed son of Śiva and his wife Parvatī, who is the remover of obstacles; Sūrya is the solar deity invoked in early Vedic hymns and still honored in morning ritual ablutions; and Śakti is the goddess Power, who may take form as the consort of each male deity as well as the great warrior goddess.

Paramātmā. In reality, worship of any deity is worship of Bhagavān. This is the established teaching (*siddhānta*) of the *śāstras.*

## Teaching #69

### There is no sin in changing one's guru

ॐ

Some people say that once you have taken up a guru you should not change to another guru. But this is not an established teaching (*siddānta*) of the *śāstras*, but rather a mental concoction. One takes a guru for one's own welfare. As long as one has not realized Bhagavat,[139] one's guru can be changed. We should not see any devotee of a guru who out of fear of taking on a new guru must remain studying in his guru's class. Just as one might take a different [school] class, so changing your guru is natural (*svabhāvika*). A former guru is not insulted; he will still be respected as a guru. But to advance in learning, one must accept discipleship to new gurus.

Śukadeva, son of Vyāsa, first acquired knowledge from his father, then he learned from Śaṅkara (Śiva), and then he learned from Nārada. Finally, he approached Janaka to take discipleship. Therefore, [the idea] "I have taken up with one guru, and so I will not take another"— such an idea is completely worthless, and is an obstacle to our welfare. One should not waste one's life by accepting this completely ridiculous argument. Countless lives have been spent wandering in various births like this, and so now, after obtaining human birth, you should be careful. Learning the nature of spiritual practice from higher and

---

[139] This is an abstract rather than personal form, translatable as the divine.

higher gurus, and carrying out all your actions according to the Veda and *śāstras*, worship Bhagavān with *bhajans* and *pūjā*, and it is certain that you will cross the ocean of *saṃsāra*.

## *Teaching #70*

**You may obtain all the knowledge available in the world, but if you do not know about yourself, you will remain ignorant**

ॐ

*Saṃsāra* is like a storeroom filled with soot. The more you associate with it, the blacker you become. Whatever the object, so act accordingly. Take action according to your intention, carry on daily activities, but don't love *saṃsāra*.

The objects of *saṃsāra* are not obstacles, rather your love for them is an obstacle. The people of *saṃsāra* are not worthy of your attachment, [so] increase your attachment instead to Paramātmā.

First learn about yourself and then try to learn about Paramātmā. If you cannot know about your self, and yet know *saṃsāra*, you will still remain ignorant. What is the use of learning about another while staying ignorant of oneself? To accumulate garbage in your own house, and then trying to clean someone else's house, cannot be intelligent at all. The day you begin learning about yourself is the very day that the poverty of your mind will disappear, and you will experience happiness and peace.

## *Teaching #71*

### By forgetting your nature you get submerged in the sea of sorrow

ॐ

Just once take a look and think, "Who are you?" Whatever you have experienced in *saṃsāra*, all that is different from you. Body, mind, intellect, breath and so on—all that you consider as your own—it's said, "my body, my mind, my intellect, my breath." Clearly, you are master of these things you consider yourself, but your existence is different from them, like your house, or your temple. The temple is yours; but you are not the temple. Similarly, body, mind, intellect, and breath and so on are yours, but you are not them. You are different from them. You are a part of Being, Consciousness, and Bliss (*sat chit ānanda*)—Paramātmā—but due to lack of discrimination, due to ignorance, you have built up such a strong association with the body-mind-intellect *(śarira, mana, buddhi*) and so forth that you have started thinking these things to be your true form.

Even if you lose a hand or leg or a sense organ, you will still live, and should an organ of knowledge such as an eye or ear be lost, then you just become blind or deaf. Your existence is not ended by the loss of an organ of action or knowledge. When you are suffering from a very painful disease, then you might say, "If I breathe my last, I'll be happy," meaning you understand that all *saṃsāra*'s pains will come to and end when your life breath leaves. Thus even the life's breath is different from you; you are not the life's breath. Whatever we see and can experience, we are nevertheless different from all of them. Understand that whatever you can forsake is different from you — our true form is that which you cannot abandon. You are a part of that permanent consciousness, *sat chit ānanda*, Paramātmā, whose true form is purity, intelligence, and freedom, the witness and experiencer of all. When we experience that our true form is different from all the world — body, senses, breath, and so on — then even while living in *saṃsāra*, one will be freed of sorrow and grief.

To experience your own form, have faith in the Vedas and *śāstra*, and having accepted the aid of a true guru, practice according to his instructions.

## *Teaching #72*

### Chant the name of Bhagavān according to rule

ॐ

People generally spend some time worshipping in one form or another, but without knowing the proper rules, the results could be the opposite [one intends] and unfavorable. First one should know the proper source for learning how to do spiritual practice (*upāsanā*). We should not just take up something from wherever we happen to find and see something, but we should take it from where the *śāstras* tell us.

When you want an heir you don't just pick up any child where you might find him. You have to marry according to the rules and regulations, go through the rituals of pregnancy, and only then will you have an heir who will be appropriate.

In this way, any work which is done, if according to ritual law, will produce the best results. This saying is completely disastrous: "Take superior knowledge, even if it comes from the low."

This saying comes from the time when pot-makers, oil-sellers and the like were becoming teachers.[140] Before, the highest wisdom could never go to the low, and if it did, he could not remain low. How can highest wisdom and lowness coexist — where light can shine, no darkness remains.

When you want to drink Ganges water, why drink from a gutter? Why not drink directly from the river currents? If you want a child, then why not give birth to a legitimate one? If you want right knowledge, then why not take it from the highest place?

## *Teaching #73*

### Chanting of the syllable Om

ॐ

Many people, barely glancing at the rules of the *śāstra* and without considering their suitability or unsuitability, will begin a spiritual practice after reading or hearing about its greatness from somewhere or another. Some people, thinking that the chanting of the syllable om is a very powerful meditation, start practicing its chanting on their own. In the *Bhagavad Gītā*, Bhagavān certainly said, "I am in the syllable om."[141] But if you want to meditate on the true form of Bhagavān for that reason, then why not catch and keep a lion? Because that, after

[140] Guru Dev uses the term *sīkṣaka*, teacher.

[141] *Bhagavad Gītā* 7.8, 9.17; see also 8.13.

all, is also the true form of Bhagavān. Bhagavān Śri Kṛṣṇachandra said, [Sanskrit:] *mṛgānāṁ ca mṛgendro 'haṃ*।[142]

I will tell you from my own experience what happens to those who, having been inspired by the greatness of chanting om, do that practice alone; listen up.

If the repetition of the syllable om is done twice, four times, or even twenty times daily, nothing special will happen. But if two or four thousand repetitions of om are done daily, then within a short period worldly tendencies will become weakened. Arsenic is poison, but if it is eaten in small quantities, nothing will happen that quickly. But just a little too much will be fatal. Similarly, if repetition of om is done in large quantities, with concentration and devotion, then worldly tendencies will definitely be weakened. One's daily earnings will be reduced, one's wife and children may become sick, and some may even die.

Five or six years ago I had gone to Lucknow for the sacrifice called *Lakṣa Chaṇḍī*. At that time, an old lady came up to me, accompanied by a few people. Those people told me that this Mata Ji was a great devotee, she carried out worship, japa, etc., the whole day, but they said that a few days previously her two grown sons had died. In reply to this I asked, "Are you chanting the syllable om?" She said, "O Maharaj! That is my very support, I chant it all day." I said, "Ok, you have destroyed *saṃsāra* through chanting, now don't abandon it. " But it will destroy that thing to which you are attached; that is the result of chanting this syllable om.

---

[142] *Bhagavad Gītā* 10.30c: "among beasts, I am the lord of beasts [the lion]."

This is the reason why householders are not permitted to do the chanting of om alone. Looking out for their welfare, the scriptures do not grant them permission. If chanting the syllable om were good for householders, then there would be no reason for the scriptures to prohibit it for them. The syllable om is prefixed to *mantras* for the purpose of auspiciousness. But another point is that ladies are prohibited to use a *mantra* with the om syllable. Where men are given *mantras* starting with om, women are given *mantras* starting with *śrī*.

Bhagavān Śaṅkara, while giving instructions to Parvatī, said that chanting *mantras* with the om syllable is like poison for a woman, and chanting *mantras* without the om syllable is auspicious for women. One should understand that Śaṅkara a ji was advising his own wife, but he kept her from the om syllable. If the om syllable would have benefited the female class, then why wouldn't Śaṅkara ji have taught it to his own better half?

## *Teaching #74*

### Guruhood is not for the Kṣatriya, Vaiśya, Śūdra, or Women

ॐ

The *śāstras* do not mention guruhood for women. Gārgī, Chuḍālā, Sulabhā, and so on, were all wise ones (*jñānīs*) as well as *yogis*. But nowhere is it found that they had made anyone their disciple.

By doing *bhajan* and worship of Bhagavān, when one's spiritual program is complete, then all can obtain knowledge, because everyone is eligible to practice devotion to Bhagavān, but not all can become gurus. Guruhood is only for the Brahmin. Along with Brahmins, the Kṣatriyas, Vaiśyas, and Śūdras can all become disciples, but not gurus. Women are also not authorized to become gurus.

King Janaka Videha was a very great wise man, but because he was a Kṣatriya, he never tried to become a guru. When Śukadeva was sent by his father Vyāsa to Janaka to learn wisdom, Janaka inquired, "Why have you come?" Śukadeva ji said, "My father sent me to take discipleship and learn from you. " King Janaka replied, "You are a Brahmin, I am a Kṣatriya, so I am not authorized to teach you. So how can I teach you when it would be against the *śāstras*?"

Then Śukadeva said, "You are a Kṣatriya, so to give charity is your *dharma*. The *śāstras* have given you permission to give charity; give the knowledge of *Brahman*[143] to me as charity. " After listening to this, Janaka seated Śukadeva on a higher seat than his own, worshipped him, and in the form of charity, he gave him the knowledge of *Brahman*. But Janaka did not make him his student to teach it. This is the ideal of those capable people who protect the limits of the *śāstras*. Nowadays *Kāyasths*, *Vaiśyas*, oil sellers, and even liquor merchants put on the different colored garb of a *sādhū* and are eager to make other their own disciples. In this way both the guru and disciple will have their downfall. These things I am saying are said in accord with the *śāstras*, I am not telling you my own mental concoction.

---

[143] Viz., *Brahmavidyā*. *Brahman* is the term for the ultimate ground of being, Godhead.

# Teaching #75

**Women benefit only by fulfilling their wifely duties**

ॐ

Women's true nature (*svabhāva*) is characterized by an excess of the *rajas guṇa*. That is why generally, they are not able to advance successfully toward *dhyāna* and *samādhi*.[144] Therefore for them there is the teaching to fulfill one's spiritual duty through devotion to their husbands. Then, by constantly tending her husband, at the time of her death, the woman will leave her body, and her next birth will be as a man. This is according to the doctrine that whatever state the individual soul entertains at the time of abandoning the body, the individual soul will manifest that very state in its next birth.

[Sanskrit:] *yaṁ yaṁ vāpismarana bhāvaṁ, tyajatyante kalevaram* |

*taṁ tamevaiti kaunteya, sadā tadbhāva bhāvitaḥ* ||[145]

If a woman leaves the body while remembering the name of Bhagavān, then she will meet Bhagavān, there is no doubt about it. But because of the predominance of the *rajas guṇa* in women's material nature (*prakṛti*), there is excessive instability in them. Therefore to keep focused on the true form of Bhagavān is difficult for them. On the other hand, it is natural for women to think about men. This is why serving the husband, remaining emotionally immersed in the husband, is said in the *śāstra* to be best for them. If a woman serves her husband and at death leaves the body thinking of her husband, will obtain a male

---

[144] *Dhyāna*, meditation, is one of the steps of *yogic* practice, as is the more difficult step of *samādhi*, sustained meditation or concentration.

[145] *Bhagavad Gītā* 8.6,"Whatever state of being one remembers when leaving the body, O son of Kuntī, one always will attain that very state."

birth and in the next birth, having fixed herself on Bhagavān, will meet Bhagavān.

The female birth is a very difficult birth. Pregnancy and childbirth is similar to the great, terrible pains of death. After that, the difficulty they suffer further in nourishing the child and caring for it can only be known by other women. No one else can begin to imagine a similar difficulty like it. Thus to be freed from the female birth which is characterized by such troubles, and to gain a male body in the next birth, the *śāstras* have given such rules for vows of devotion to one's husband. This is for the benefit of all women.

## *Teaching #76*

### Act according to the Veda and *śāstra* which are Bhagavān's orders

ॐ

People spare no effort to become wealthy and have children, but they do not make comparable efforts to become wise. If one becomes wise, a person will obtain all happiness and peace. However, not just anyone who is called a guru can be called an *ācharyā*. Only someone who has all the qualities of an *ācharyā* can be regarded as an *ācharyā*. Only one who is already an *ācharyā* can make another an *ācharyā*.

[Sanskrit:] *śruti-smṛti mamaivājñe, yastoṁllaṅghya vartate* |

*ājñocchedī mamadrohī, madbhaktopi na me priyaḥ* ||[146]

This means, "*śruti* and *smṛti* are my commandments. If anyone transgresses these, he becomes my enemy, and is not dear to me even if he be my devotee."

Hence *śruti* and *smṛti* (Veda and *śāstra*) should be considered primary, as they are the orders of Bhagavān.

The teaching I am giving here is strictly according to the Veda and *śāstra*; it is not someone's mental concoction. I never advise anyone to just follow my words. If you start listening to my personal opinions, then you will become accustomed to listening to the Śāṅkarācharyā. If a foolish person should eventually happen to attain this seat, you will listen to him as well. Following someone's personal opinions will not lead to any good, only minding the words of the Veda and *śāstra* will. Therefore, I say do not make a habit of listening to a Śāṅkarācharyā's personal opinions, but instead listen to the Veda and *śāstra*. The *śāstras* say that the Veda *śāstra* is the commandment of Bhagavān.

The devotees of Bhagavān must definitely mind the Veda and *śāstra* which are the commandments of Bhagavān. As long as one has not realized Bhagavān, it is necessary to follow their instructions. When you realize Bhagavān, then you yourself will attain divine form (*Bhagavatrupa*); and at that time, there will be no question of following orders.

---

[146] Guru Dev's quote is an interesting variant of *Viṣṇudharma* 76.31. Translation and source from Mudumby Narasimhachary, *ISKCON Communication Journal*, Vol 8, No 2, March 2001, "Interpretation as a Means of Understanding Tradition: A Srivaisnava Perspective."

# Teaching #77

### Who is a "Guru"?

[Sanskrit:] *tad vijñānārthaṁ—sagurumevābhigacchet* ।,

*samitpāṇiḥ śrotriyaṁ brahmaniṣṭham* ॥[147]

Here every word has two meanings. One is the direct meaning (*vācyārtha*) of the words, and the other is its implied meaning (*lakṣyārtha*).

ॐ

In this teaching, the direct meaning of the word *tat* is *mayopādhi caitanya deva īśvara*,[148] Bhagavān Rāma, Kṛṣṇa, Śakti, and so on, who are *Brahman* with form (*sākāra*). The implied meaning of *tat* is complete *Brahman*, who is beyond *māyā*, the attributeless (*nirguṇa*), formless (*nirākāra*) Paramātmā, who pervades all animate and inanimate forms. Thus *tat* represents Paramātmā with form and with attributes (*saguṇa*), and in the implied sense the formless, attributeless Parambrahma as well. One who is interested in deeply understanding this should go to a guru. He should not approach the guru empty-handed. One should take some fruit and flowers.

One should approach only a guru who is *śrotriya*, and is *brahmaniṣṭha*. The meaning of *śrotriya* is one who has fully understood the meaning of Vedas and *śāstras*, and we call someone *brahmaniṣṭha* who through the Vedas and

---

[147] *Muṇḍaka Upaniṣad* Book 1, Chapter 2, second half of verse 12. Guru Dev does not directly translate this Sanskrit verse into Hindi, choosing instead to offer an extended commentary. This portion of the Sanskrit verse means, "Let him, in order to understand this, with fuel offering in hand, approach a guru who is fully learned and firmly rooted in *Brahman*."

[148] "The intelligent divine lord with the attribute of *māyā*."

Vedārtha is fixed on and enjoys Parabrahma Paramātmā.[149] Only one who has both these qualities can be called a guru and *āchārya.*

The guru is a boat that crosses the ocean of being. It is very rare to get a Sat guru in *saṃsāra*, and yet everything is easily attained here, too. Vedas and *śāstras* are full of *mantras*, there is no shortage of *mantras*. However, the *mantras* given in books are like a heap of bullets. There may be hundreds of varieties of bullets piled up, and one may also have a gun, but they will be useless unless someone can advise us which caliber to use from among the pile of bullets. As a skilled hunter uses different caliber bullets to hunt a lion, an elephant, or a deer, similarly only an experienced guru knows which *mantras* are to be given to whom. Having observed the capacity and inclination, and so on, of a disciple, and in accordance with their eligibility, he determines *mantras* which would be beneficial and would benefit devotees.

Nowhere in the scriptures do we find a teaching that gurus should go to their disciples. Nowhere do we find a teaching that disciples should send a car to bring their guru; disciples should go to their guru, this is respectable. However, since gurus have come to depend on their disciples for their livelihood, guruhood's respectability has been besmirched. Who is a *rāj guru* (royal guru)? They are *rāj goru.* A *goru* is an animal. Such a guru, like a king, will have a lot of property, he will begin riding in cars, and what's more, he enjoys all heavenly comforts, so now he drops his own *puruṣārtha.* He stops thinking about the welfare of his disciples, and does not bother even if they are bound for hell. Tulasīdās had rightly written:

---

[149] The literal meaning of *brahmaniṣṭha* is "firmly rooted in *Brahman.*"

*harai śiṣya dhana, śoka na haraī* | *Mau guru ghora naraka maṁha paraī* ||[150]

How can sorrow be removed? The *śruti* says, *tarati śokam ātmavit.*[151] The one who knows the self crosses the ocean of sorrow. Thus when a disciple approaches a person who is well-versed in the scriptures and is firmly established in *Brahman*, he will attain knowledge of the self. This is an instruction given by *śruti*.

If the guru cannot give knowledge of the self (*ātma jñāna*) to the disciple, or if he fails to make him see Bhagavān, but instead continues to take his money, then he will definitely go to a terrible hell. If I accept someone as my disciple, then I work hard to help him obtain the knowledge of the Self or to have vision of Bhagavān. If the disciple is incapable of accomplishing this due to his own unfitness, only then am I saved from going to hell. Knowing this, I do not take any financial or other services from any disciple whatsoever.

Once I was at the Kumbha Mela in Prayaga [Allahabad]. There during one of the meetings I said, "I've been thinking—my shop is new, but it is going very well." Having heard this, some sādhus said, "There aren't any transactions. This must be a sarcastic remark at our expense." Thinking this, some people came to me and asked, "Maharaj, in a store there is buying and selling, but you are not involved in transactions. So what do you mean by your statement?" I replied, "I also give and take, but my transactions are different from yours. You people all deal in money, but I deal in something more valuable."

---

150 Guru Dev renders into modern standarad Hindi some of the verses by Tulasīdās that were originally composed in Avadhi, a variant of Hindi.

151 Literally, "the knower of *ātman* crosses sorrow." *Chāndogya Upaniṣad* 7.1.3.

Consider how when two wealthy persons are in a dispute, they are ready to sacrifice their entire property to win the case, but neither will bend before the other. Whatever happens, they will not bow their head before anyone else. This very head that they refuse to bow even at the cost of their complete destruction, they will bring and touch to the very floor before me. They have nothing more valuable than this bowing of their head to give me. In this way, we take their most precious offering and in return give them the path that will lead to their good welfare. This is our transaction. What is meant by bowing the head can be understood only by that person who had never bowed his head before anyone. One whose head bows this way and that way — he does not know the value of bowing his head, and such persons value money more than this. Bowing the head represents surrendering the ego[152] and surrendering one's own existence. It is wrong to consider money as more valuable than this. We take people's ego and give them the path that leads to their good welfare, this is thus our kind of transaction.

## *Teaching #78*

### Who is called a *Jagad Guru*?

ॐ

In *saṃsāra*, we find two types of people — theists and atheists. In the atheist world, there is no guru. The gurus in the [theist] world should be called *Jagad Guru*. We find two types of faith among theists. Some people have faith in

---

[152] *Ahaṃkāra*, literally, "I-maker."

the manifest aspect of *Brahman* and some have faith in the unmanifest aspect of *Brahman*. Only one who has the capability to become a guru for both the manifest-believers and unmanifest-believers can be called a *Jagad Guru.*

The explanation for this is that among the gods with form, there are five supported by the Vedas: Viṣṇu, Śiva, Śakti, Sūrya, and Gaṇeṣa. A *Jagad Guru* is someone who can nurture knowledge of these five manifest gods, and can also teach those who do not have faith in these five manifest deities, but instead espouse the unmanifest and formless. Those who teach the practice of just one god among the five are like doctors who can only treat a few diseases. They are like a poor medicine man who keeps vials of medicine for different diseases; he doesn't even have the status of a compounder, and yet he might call himself a civil surgeon.[153] Who can stop someone from giving his son the name of Rām? But one doesn't become Rām[154] merely by having that name. Similarly, if someone writes *Jagad Guru* at the beginning of his name, who can stop them? But when you start asking to see a true *Jagad Guru*, then the one who bears the mark of a *Jagad Guru* is he from whose door no devotee of any god leaves disappointed. In modern times, the different sects[155] have hierarchized spiritual practice devoted to Śiva, Śakti, Viṣṇu, etc., which is improper. Among these five gods, there is none smaller or greater than the other. Every god is capable of benefiting his devotee in the same way, and therefore every worshipper is Vaiṣṇava, because every god is an aspect of the supreme Bhagavān. Bhagavān himself has explained:

---

[153] The English words "compounder" and "civil surgeon" are both in the original.

[154] Viz., "God." Rām is a very popular name among Hindus.

[155] A *sampradāya* is a lineage of devotees who follow the teachings of a specific spiritual leader.

[Sanskrit:] *jñānaṁ gaṇeśo mama cakṣurarkaḥ,*

*śivo mamātmā mamaśaktirādyā* I

*vibheda buddhayā mayi ye bhajanti,*

*mamāṅgahīnaṁ kalayanti mandāḥ* II

Gaṇeśa is Bhagavān's head, Sūrya is his eyes, Śiva is his *ātman*, Ādyabhagavatī is his Śakti. Thus if someone does not consider these five gods to be the different parts of the body of Bhagavān, and practice with the attitude of difference, then he is not worshipping Bhagavān, but butchering his limbs.

It is very clear that whoever denies[156] Gaṇeśa, even if a devotee of Viṣṇu, is cutting the head off Bhagavān Viṣṇu. If a Viṣṇu devotee denies Śiva, then he is cutting off the soul of Bhagavān Viṣṇu. Similarly, one who denies Devī renders Bhagavān powerless. Thus, those people of today's sects who envy and hate others, and call themselves Vaiṣṇavas, or those who worship Śiva and call themselves Śaivas and refute Bhagavān Viṣṇu, are neither Vaiṣṇava nor Śaiva—they are just conceited. A Vaiṣṇava is one who is a devotee of Bhagavān Viṣṇu—

[Sanskrit:] *viṣṇaurataḥ vaiṣṇavāḥ ūrdhvaṁpuṇḍvatvaṁ* I[157]

A Vaiṣṇava is said to be one who wears a vertical sign. This is not a definitive teaching (*siddhānta*).

Anyone who worships Viṣṇu is a Vaiṣṇava. But anyone who worships any deity can also be called a Vaiṣṇava. Whenever anyone does the spiritual

---

[156] Guru Dev is making a pun here, for the phrase *khandan karaṇa* mean literally to segment or break into pieces, but its connotation is to refute, contradict, or deny.

[157] Literally, a Vaiṣṇava is a person who wears vertical sectarian marks.

practice of any god, he becomes a Vaiṣṇava. The entire theistic world is Vaiṣṇava.

Those who think that by applying vertical marks and calling oneself Vaiṣṇava and calling others non-Vaiṣṇava are out of touch with reality. They are insulting Viṣṇu. Similarly, if any spiritual practitioner of Śiva or Śakti thinks that he is not a Vaiṣṇava, then it is also his mistake. In *saṃsāra*, there is no one who is not a Vaiṣṇava. The communalist rhetoric of sectarian spokesmen isn't helpful to them or to others.

## *Teaching #79*

### Reflecting on conversations with the pious is necessary

ॐ

Śukadeva expounded the *Bhāgavata* [*Purāṇa*] and thousands of people heard, but only Parikṣit achieved *mokṣa* from it. Many listened to Gokarṇa, too, but only Dhundhakārī achieved *mokṣa*. The question naturally arises: when there is abundant rain everywhere, why is just one man's thirst quenched? The answer is that *mokṣa* depends on the mind. Whatever one dwells on, then the mental impression of that thought is strengthened, and the bondage or freedom of a *jīva* depends on it. *Śruti* and *smṛiti* give the established doctrines:

[Sanskrit:] *mana eva manuṣyānām kāranaṁ bandhamokṣayoḥ* ||[158]

*dhyāna eva manuṣyānām kāranaṁ bandhamokṣayoḥ* ||[159]

---

[158] Viz., "Verily, the mind itself binds or releases human beings."

We should continuously ponder and reflect on whatever doctrines or teachings about the divine we hear in the company of the pious.

By listening to the words of the pious, one's ears will be purified. But if no further contemplation is done on those words, they will remain only there in the ear or they will go in one ear and out the other. The basic purpose of *satsaṅga* is to purify the mind. Mind is the primary thing here. If the mind remains impure, the life and death cycle will continue. If instead the mind becomes pure, one attains liberation. Maharishi Yājñavālkya says that *dhyāna* (meditation, concentration) is the cause for either liberation or bondage. Meditation is possible only by the mind. If the mind becomes pure, it starts meditating on Bhagavān and thus man will attain liberation. But if the mind remains impure, it gets entangled in bad tendencies (*vāsanā*) and will have futile worries, and start concentrating on unnecessary things. Thus, it keeps one wandering in the circle of *saṃsāra*.

## *Teaching #80*

### Become a *mahātma* even while residing at home

ॐ

One can become a *mahātma* wherever one lives. No one becomes a *mahātma* by simply wearing ocher clothing or by applying some marks on one's forehead. Dress is not beneficial — auspicious welfare comes from faith. The state of a *māhātma* is decided by the state of mind. So stay wherever you are, but

---

[159] Viz.,"Verily, meditation itself binds or releases human beings."

change the direction of your mind. Decrease your thoughts of *saṃsāra*, and increase your thoughts of Paramātmā.

Nowadays people stress thinking about what one should not [waste time] thinking about. One should primarily contemplate Paramātmā; instead, people contemplate objects of *saṃsāra*. That is why they are not able to experience peace and happiness. If protecting one's vital breath (*prāṇa*) is dedicated to just worldly activities and enjoyment of the senses, then it is nothing more than the bellows of a blacksmith. Hence take care of your vital breath and apply yourself to Paramātmā.

First generate faith (*śraddhā*). You already have sufficient faith in money. That is why you are able to think about it. When you have faith in Paramātmā, then you will start contemplating him. You must realize that money and all the objects of *saṃsāra* will remain here, while you have to carry out your future journey alone. Prepare for that future journey at this very moment. Increase your faith in higher goals, and increase your love for that ever-blissful Paramātmā. Show merely courteous interest in the things of the world that will always remain here, and place primary faith in the ultimate goal, which will accompany you.

Once you figure out that a tantalizing horde of money has actually just been fashioned by a magician, temptation to take it will wither, and you'll be unable to love it. Like the magician's money, all the objects and relationships of *saṃsāra* are transient. So carry out all your daily affairs according to societal expectations. But do not reserve a place for these things in your mind. In your mind, reserve place for the imperishable Paramātmā, whose very essence is bliss. Always keep the memory of Bhagavān in your mind and never transgress the bounds of propriety — this is what it means to be a *Māhātma*.

## *Teaching #81*

**It is more important to purify the intellect than to accumulate wealth**

ॐ

Your children will benefit greatly if you put half of the effort you put into accumulating wealth into purifying your intellect.

If the intellect is pure, then even with less wealth, children will experience greater peace and happiness. If the intellect is evil, however, then even with unlimited wealth and property, one's children will become entangled in bad mental dispositions (*durvāsanā*) and they will experience only unhappiness and sorrow. Therefore, first try to purify your intellect, and then earn wealth.

## *Teaching #82*

**Without knowledge (*jnāna*) there can be neither *Bhakti* nor *Mokṣa***

ॐ

Many births are required to work out the *karma* generated during one human lifetime. That is why the *jīva* must experience such a large balance of accumulated *karma*. To exhaust it all would take innumerable births. If the *jīva* wants to exhaust all this accumulated *karma* through experience, as long as accumulated *karma* is undestroyed, then one cannot free oneself from the cycle of birth and death. But the fire of knowledge has been born that can exhaust the huge mound of accumulated *karma* instantly. The awakened ones call the person who has burned all accumulated *karma* with the help of the fire of knowledge a *paṇḍit*.

[Sanskrit:] *jñānāgni dagdhakarmāṇam tamāhuḥ paṇḍitaṁ budhāḥ* ||[160]

If someone kills another within the flash of an angry minute, he will either be hanged or receive a very long prison term. By way of this example, we can see that the *karma* of an action that occurs over just two to four minutes can take many years to work off. Just think how many births it will require to work off the *karma* from the actions done in the span of one entire life. This shows the greatness of the knowledge that can destroy accumulated (*sañcita*) *karma*.

[Sanskrit:] *yathaidhāṁsi samiddhognir bhasmasātkurute 'rjuna* |

*jñānāgni sarvakarmāṇi bhasmasātkurute tathā* ||[161]

This means that just as the fire's flame burns all traces of fuel to ashes, the fire of knowledge burns up all accumulated *karma*. Therefore destroy accumulated *karma* with the fire of knowledge and experience currently manifesting (*prārabdha*) *karma* peacefully.

To acquire that knowledge which can burn up all accumulated *karma* is the highest goal. After gaining that knowledge, there will be nothing left to be done.

[Sanskrit:] *jñānāmṛtena tṛptasya kṛtakṛtyasya yoginaḥ* |

*naivāsti kiṁcitkartavyaṁ asti cennasa tattvavit* ||

For the knowledgeable one, it is written, "If he desires something, then he should chant the om syllable for it."

---

[160] Viz., He whose actions have been burnt in the fire of knowledge is called by the awakened "paṇḍitam." *Bhagavad Gītā* 4.19cd.

[161] *Bhagavad Gītā* 4.37.

[Sanskrit:] *buddha tatvena dhī doṣa śūnyenekāntavāsinaḥ* I

*dīrghaṁ praṇavamuccārya manorājyaṁ vilīyate* II

After gaining knowledge, one obtains *videha mokṣa* once released from the body.[162] But for *jīvanmukti*, one must take recourse in the practice of grasping the self.

First there is *aparokṣa* knowledge, that is, that knowledge which becomes clear from the study of the *śāstra* and gurus: that one, unique Paramātmā, which is all pervasive everywhere in all creation, who is being, consciousness, and bliss, and the very embodiment of unbounded knowledge. This type of certainty — wisdom devoid of doubt — is *aparokṣa* knowledge.

Prahalāda knew from the beginning that, "My Rām is fully immanent in all, everywhere." He was certain, so day and night he dwelled on thoughts of Bhagavān. Until one knows Bhagavān, how can one perform his *bhakti*? To accept that Bhagavān is everywhere in creation is knowledge, and to apply oneself to his service and devotion is *bhakti*. *Vijñāna* is seeing him appear in one place directly through *bhakti*, and after *vijñāna*, to become absorbed in that state is supreme devotion (*parābhakti*).

---

[162] *Videha mokṣa*, literally, "bodiless release," is the state of release attained only after the body is cast off. This is in contrast with *jīvanmukti*, enlightenment while still living an embodied existence.

## *Teaching #83*

**Hasten to do good works**

ॐ

The *jīva* has been experiencing *saṃsāra* for many, many births. It is only natural, therefore, that its tendencies (*pravṛtti*) have become oriented toward *saṃsāra*. To turn its tendency toward Paramātmā and away from *saṃsāra* requires effort. In reality, the aim of life is to stop the mind from involvement with *saṃsāra*. If one engages in the spiritual practice of Bhagavān and thinking and speaking about him, the mind will start dwelling on him, and after some time, it will withdraw from *saṃsāra* on its own.

In our daily affairs we should adopt a strategy of trying to complete good works as well as works related to the divine quickly. Should any wrong thought arise, on the other hand, we should try to postpone it to another time by saying, "I'll do it tomorrow, or the day after next." In this way, [negative impulses] can be continuously postponed.

## *Teaching #84*

**If you want to benefit from Bhagavān, then do spiritual practice and make him manifest in one location**

ॐ

The all-pervasive, formless divine being (*bhagavatsattā*) is incapable of action; it is merely a witness. Only when it manifests itself in one place with the help of *māyā* can it take some action in *māyā's* world, characterized as it is by the three *guṇas*. This is like the fire which remains unmanifest in wood; even though it is all-pervading, it cannot light the wood, nor can it perform any act. But when wood is rubbed, the wood can burn and act as we desire. Similarly, when the all-pervasive divine being manifests in some site with the help of our spiritual practice, then there can be some worldly benefit.

Spiritual practice is a staircase by which the devotee climbs to Bhagavān, and Bhagavān climbs down to the devotee. Only by spiritual practice does the being of Bhagavān, which abides in all animate and inanimate things, manifest itself in one site and thus acts in accordance with the devotee's desires. Only when the formless, unmanifest pure existence manifests itself in a form with attributes can any activity take place. Hence if you want to receive Bhagavān's blessings, then carry out spiritual practice and make him manifest, either inside or outside. Once Bhagavān manifests in one's heart, only then will all the poverty of life be eliminated.

## *Teaching #85*

### If you want happiness, walk towards the ocean of happiness

ॐ

Something can be obtained only where it is available. If you want money, you must approach the wealthy; if you want wisdom, you must go to the wise. If you want to buy pearls and diamonds, you have to go to a jeweler's shop, because no matter how hard you search in a vegetable market, you will not find diamonds. Similarly, if you want peace and happiness, you must approach Paramātmā, who is the essence of peace and happiness, to attain peace and happiness. However hard you may keep pounding your head against the ground, however much you labor in *saṃsāra*, you yourself will not be able to obtain peace and happiness.

As hard as you strive to gain peace and happiness by earning money and acquiring recognition, you will be handed an equal measure of sorrow and restlessness. You may imagine happiness to be something else. Say you imagine, "If I can just get this particular object, then I will be happy," then once that thing is acquired, you may think, "Now I am happy." This kind of imagining is another matter. But understand that [true] peace and happiness are found in none of the objects here.

By falling into the exuberance of *saṃsāra*, you have forgotten the Paramātmā, who is unlimited and full of bliss. Because you have distanced yourself from Īśvara, you have become unhappy, and that unhappiness will leave only in his presence. You have lost yourself so much in the things of the world that you have become deluded about your very nature. You do not know, "Who am I?"

What can be said about a madman who is so insane that he has forgotten his own identity and cannot recognize his own true form? Such a person seeks light in a dark cave; searching for peace and happiness in things of *saṃsāra* is like the man desiring light, but entering a dark cave.

If you want happiness, then approach Paramātmā who is the ocean of happiness. Only by approaching Paramātmā can you obtain peace, happiness, and glory for this world and the next. As darkness surrounds a person bereft of light, so unhappiness and troubles surround a person who turns away from Paramātmā

## *Teaching #86*

### Pray to Bhagavān without fail, whether the mind likes it or not

ॐ

If you remember Bhagavān, even with an impure and wicked mind, your sins will be destroyed, just as you will burn yourself when you touch a flame, whether you wanted to touch it or not. To love Bhagavān is difficult because the mind has rotted after so many lifetimes in the past. Sit to do *bhajans* without fail. If the mind wants to run here and there, let it run, but don't get up and run after it. Sit to do *bhajans* and do not worry if your mind wanders. Continue to sit counting each round on the rosary with that very mind. Don't think, "My mind is too scattered," and then get up. The mind can develop concentration gradually, and you should not worry. But one thing is essential to pay attention to, and that is to continue the *bhajans* to Bhagavān, yet at the same time, guard against committing sins. Do not think, "Since prayer to Bhagavān destroys sins, why can't I commit just a few more?" If you begin committing sins, those very sins will draw you away from your prayer to Bhagavān—this is certain.

## *Teaching #87*

### Is it best to experience *darśan* of Bhagavān through knowledge (jñāna) or through perception?

ॐ

[Seeing Bhagavān] happens in two ways. In whatever way he comes before you, and in whatever form he appears, visualize that very form — don't resist. If He comes to you in a manifest form, then visualize him in that form, and if He remains in an unmanifested state, then be strong in your faith. But for everyday purposes, you should choose one spiritual practice as a base and follow its rules. Basing oneself on a particular practice clarifies. To keep faith in only the formless state, the mind must be transformed into an eye that sees. It is necessary to adopt and follow a particular spiritual practice. Through spiritual practice and meditating, love for one's chosen deity increases, and when love increases, the chosen one is realized directly.

## *Teaching #88*

### Don't get involved in any controversy over *bhakti* and *jñāna*, or arguments about the manifest (*sākār*) and unmanifest (*nirākār*)

ॐ

People discuss many concepts related to *bhakti* and *jñāna*. Some argue that knowledge is superior, and some that *bhakti* is. Only those who don't know the true meaning of *bhakti* and *jñāna* feel this way, because they see *bhakti* and knowledge to be opposed, and are willing to fight over it. It has been said that to know Paramātmā is *jñāna*, and, having known Him, to worship Him is *bhakti*.

If you don't know Him, then how can you worship Him? You see, it is very clear that without knowledge, *bhakti* is not possible. Neither those who are against *jñāna* and in favor of *bhakti*, nor those who favor *jñāna* but oppose *bhakti*, are aware of their own spiritual blindness. How can one trust the testimony of the blind? We can only trust the words of someone with sight.

Some people fight over the distinction between the manifest and the unmanifest. If you believe that Paramātmā is almighty, then how can you say, "He isn't manifest," or "He remains unmanifest." Believing that Paramātmā is almighty, to say that "He is unmanifest," and "He is not manifest" is a complete contradiction. When you say Paramātmā is completely free and independent, then how it is not possible for him to take *any* form, or to think he is not able to do something? To explain Bhagavān as existing with qualities and without, I would like to give an example. Fire is everywhere. Fire is even in water, fire is in every solid thing, fire is in wood. There is no place where fire does not exist. We know without doubt that fire is all pervasive. As fire, Paramātmā is all-pervasive.

Fire exists unmanifest even in a splinter of wood. If you put the splinter into the fireplace and pray for it to burn, it will not. Until fire takes form from formlessness, it can be of no use. Fire may exist without qualities, but [in this state] it will be useless for you. Similarly, the unqualified, unmanifest Parabrahma is all-pervasive in all creation, and like the unmanifest fire, it is useless to you. If anything is to be accomplished in this world, it will only be done by the manifest *Brahman*. With the help of the guru, the disciple can light the splinter from within and make use of this manifest form as he sees fit. As long as Bhagavān does not manifest himself in some form from formlessness, He can do absolutely nothing for us. In the same context, the *Bhagavad Gītā* says

[Sanskrit:] *yadā yadā hi dharmasya glānir bhavati bhārata* ।

*abhyutthānam adharmasya tadātmānaṁ sṛjāmy 'ham* ॥[163]

[The phrase] "*ātmānaṁ sṛjāmi*" means "When I take form from formlessness." When? "When *dharma* is on the decline and *adharma* is on the rise." Why does the Lord have to take on a form from within the formless? It explains this by saying,

---

[163] *Bhagavad Gītā* 4.7.

[Sanskrit:] *paritrāṇāya sādhūnāṁ, vināśāya ca dūṣkṛtām* ǀ

*dharma saṁsthāpanārthāya sambhavāmi yuge yuge* ǁ[164]

"For the benefit of the good and to destroy the evil, I manifest myself and I establish *dharma*." Don't take the word sādhu here to mean those who wear ocher robes or sectarian marks on their foreheads or sacred rosaries. The meaning of the word sādhu is this — sādhus are good-natured people with good hearts, who respect the limits set by Vedas and *śāstras* and who have faith in their own enjoined duties and follow them. Bhagavān's avatars are for the welfare of those people.

If Bhagavān does not assume a manifest form, then the world cannot be orderly. The order of a thing can be maintained only within the parameters of that thing. For example, if you bring a loudspeaker[165] and place it in front of me, but I sit silently, then it will serve no purpose. The unmanifest is like me sitting silent. If I always sit silent, what benefit can there be for you all? No profit can be derived from the unmanifest Bhagavān until he assumes a form. I am telling you the way it is. I must explain these teachings strictly as they are told in the Vedas and *śāstra*, and not to expound my own thinking. My duty is to explain the teachings clearly. In this respect, I do not care whether the words are pleasing to one or irritating to another. I neither need to please nor to antagonize anybody. Still, I question those people who propound only the unmanifest. In fact, I also accept the unmanifest, but not the unmanifest alone. I ask those who propound only the formless — can any profit be derived from the unmanifest fire that is

---

[164] *Bhagavad Gītā* 4.8.

[165] The English word "loudspeaker" is in the original.

hidden in a piece of wood? Please show me any bread cooked by an unmanifest fire. The formless is only being.

I would like to ask those people who meditate only on the formless, how exactly have you meditated on the unmanifest? The mind can only concentrate on an object of meditation, so how can one make the unmanifest on object of meditation?

Concentration (*dhyāna*) is not possible on the unmanifest. If someone says that he concentrates on the formless, it is like saying that he is going to attend the wedding of the son of a barren woman. The son of a barren woman cannot exist, so how can he marry? When there is no form or outline to the unmanifest, how can one make it an object of meditation? To collect the mental formations, some foundation is necessary. Whatever is taken as the mind's foundation, that becomes the form.

Formlessness is beyond all the trios, namely: meditation, meditator, and object of mediation, and knowledge, knower, and object of knowledge. Meditation on the formless is mere mockery. Only those who do not understand the principle of formlessness can talk about meditation on the formless. The principle of formlessness is merely for understanding; it is the principle of existence, but the world cannot derive any benefit from this principle. Can anybody derive any benefit from an unmanifest son? Can anybody go to an unmanifest school and study? Can any minister[166] sit on an unmanifest chair? Can anyone cure a disease with an unmanifest medicine? Can anyone be pleased with unmanifest food? The unmanifest is a completely useless thing. It cannot be

---

[166] The English word "minister" is in the original.

used for any purpose. That is why the argument about formlessness is thoroughly useless.

The unmanifest is like a seed kept in that same form. If the seed is locked in a box, what is the use of it? But if you sow it and do all the things required to grow it, then it will give flowers and fruits. Until then, what's the benefit of a seed?

The formless Paramātmā is all-pervading everywhere. For example, consider a room full of furniture, and the unmanifest fire is within the furniture's wood. If the room becomes dark, that all-pervading unmanifest fire cannot remove it. But if some of the furniture is ignited, the unmanifest fire can be made manifest, and the darkness of that room will be eliminated immediately. But as long as the fire is not manifest, it will not be useful in the daily affairs of this manifest world. Only when the formless manifests in some form will it be useful to the world.

If Paramātmā should assume form, then is it your beast of burden, to work however you wish? He is the extremely independent. The Veda says, "[Sanskrit:] *so 'kṣaraḥ parama svarāt."* This means he is the syllable[167] that cannot be destroyed.

Paramātmā is supremely independent. Those who think, "He is the unmanifest and is not manifest," or "He is manifest, not unmanifest," have not understood the teaching about Paramātmā's essence. Taking one side or the other, they start fighting. We should not become involved in the argument about manifest and unmanifest. The One who is manifest is also the unmanifest.

---

[167] The word "syllable" or *akṣaraḥ* literally means "indivisible. "

Unmanifestness is merely for understanding and the manifest is for doing the welfare of the world.

When the unmanifest Paramātmā manifests itself, it is like the unmanifest fire, present everywhere within the wood, which only manifests as flame when we apply vigorous friction. Only then do we realize there was unmanifested fire in the wood. Similarly, when unqualified, unmanifest Paramātmā manifests itself, all our doubts about unqualified, unmanifest Paramātmā vanish. Only one who manifests fire by rubbing wood can say without doubt that fire resides in the wood. When fire manifests in form, one can be completely certain about the manifest fire in the wood. If it is not possible to produce a flame from wood, then we cannot speak about unmanifested fire in the wood with full conviction. When Bhagavān manifests himself, only then can we say with full confidence that he must exist in unmanifest form. With the help of the manifest form, we have evidence of the unmanifest. Otherwise, how can anyone know the unmanifest? As fire manifests from the state of being unqualified to the state of being qualified, so also Paramātmā manifests itself from the unqualified to the qualified. It is completely invalid to say that the qualified does not come from the unqualified. Due to groups of proponents of the unqualifed, sin has increased significantly in society, because these people don't accept the qualified Bhagavān, and they think that the unqualified cannot hear or see anything, so they act as they wish. They don't understand the meaning of sin and virtue.

# *Teaching #89*

**We must reap the consequences of what we have sown**

ॐ

Whether today, or after ten years, or after ten births, it is certain that we must reap the consequences of our actions. Whatever action is performed, large or small, there will certainly be a corresponding result. This is certain:

[Sanskrit:] *atyugra puṇyapāpānāṁ, ihaiva phalamaśnute* ।

If an action is powerful and demonstrates great virtue or great sin, then the result of that action will appear within a short time in this same birth. Actions of ordinary virtue or sin may produce their results after a longer period. But we will never escape the fruits of any of our actions.

The One who delivers the result of our action is all-knowing. Action is impersonal, likewise its result. He who administers the result of every action is the conscious Paramātmān, dwelling within all, the knower of everything and all-pervasive. He keeps perfect account of every action done by every person. According to the action, he delivers the result. You can prevent people from seeing your actions, but you cannot cast Paramātmā's eyes away. Not a single action can be done which can be kept from Paramātmā's eyes. Therefore, don't do any action which you believe to be a sin. Don't forget that sinful action is the cause of sorrow. Whatever action we do, the result of that action will return to us. If you perform right action, the result will be happiness, and if you perform wrong action, you most certainly will suffer. If you plant the seed of an acacia tree, it will bear thorns, not mangoes.

# *Teaching #90*

## Whatever is in your mind, speak and act accordingly

ॐ

In those days when I was living in the forest alone, once I stopped in a temple near Riwa, on the bank of the river in the forest. A village stood nearby. A man from there came and he worshipped in the temple, and he came and asked me, "Maharaj, knowers (*jñāni log*) attain liberation by the power of their knowledge. Devotees cross [this ocean of *saṃsāra*] by the power of their devotion, and the destitute resort to the help of Bhagavān, who is the protector of the oppressed. So which people go to hell?" I told him, "I'll give you the answer tomorrow morning."

The next morning, the man returned. He went to the temple and started praying before Bhagavān, saying,

[Sanskrit:] *pāpo 'haṁ pāpakarmā 'haṁ, pāpātmā pāpasambhavaḥ* ||

He continued praying in this fashion for quite some time — "I am sinful. My *self* is sinful. I commit evil *karma*," and so on. When he had finished, and was approaching me, I told a Brahmacāri, "Throw this sinner out. How has such a sinner come before us this morning? No one should see his face.[168] Remove this evil person quickly far away from here."

After moving a little away from me, he starting telling the Brahmacāri, "I am not as great a sinner as Maharaj thinks." When I heard this, I called to him and said, "I am not calling you a sinner; I am answering your question from yesterday."

---

[168] It is considered unlucky to see a sinner early in the morning.

"When I called you a sinner, you felt very unhappy. From this it can be understood that you do not really consider yourself a sinner. But every morning you come before Bhagavān and start saying, "I am sinful, I am a committer of evil *karma*." You were speaking this way before Bhagavān, but in your own mind you don't consider yourself to be a sinner. These type of people who believe one thing but say another, go to hell, keeping one thing in your mind, you say something different. And this is the answer to your question. People should keep the inside and outside the same; as one thinks, so should one speak, and so should one act; only then will you deceive nobody, and you also will experience happiness and peace."

## *Teaching #91*

**Do not entangle your mind in the things of this world, apply it toward Bhagavān**

ॐ

It is not correct to entangle the mind much in *saṃsāra*. You need to act with discrimination. We have only three things in life: body, mind, and wealth. If these three things are utilized properly, then there will be no occasion to repent. Let bygones be bygones, but take care that from now on you do not spoil things. If you rely on the Vedas and scriptures, then you needn't fear that you will lapse. The time will come anyway when you will have to leave this place. Therefore you should accumulate only the wealth and riches which will be useful in the next world.

Wisdom consists of using things properly. The pupose of mind is just to contemplate Bhagavān. Contemplating worldly things is a misuse.

The proper utilization of the body is for the sake of others and in carrying out *bhajan* and *pūjā* of Bhagavān. Creating trouble for others, theft, etc., are misuses of the body.

Similarly, employing wealth in good activities is its proper utilization. Using it for wrong desires is its misuse. Wealth is used for three purposes. One purpose is to spend it in charity (*dānaṃ*), another in enjoyment (*bhogo*), or else it is dissipated (*nāśaḥ*). What wealth is not enjoyed or given in charity, will end up as the third possibility, meaning it will be wasted.

There are three types of charity: *sāttvik*, *rājasik*, and *tāmasik*. *Sattvik* charity (*dāna*) gives the best results. The meaning of enjoyment here does not mean the way people are using wealth for enjoyment nowadays. An extremely luxurious life is not right. Even enjoyment must be within certain ethical limits. The mind can never be satisfied with the enjoyment of things. No one, in fact, should expect that the mind will ever be satisfied one day. Let the senses wither and be useless for any work. Even then, the mind will not be satisfied. It is just impossible to get satisfaction and contentment though enjoyment. This principle will not change if one enjoys a bit or one enjoys day in and day out. If you drink a cup of wine or ten bottles, it is the same.

If you really want to get intoxicated, get high in such a way that you never have to come down. What is the use of the ordinary way of getting high, where you lose money and even the high wears off?

The attainment of Bhagavān is such an intoxication that it doesn't wear off as soon as it comes. We should seek the kind of intoxication that never goes away, even after the body is cast off.

In human life you must base your actions on proper thinking. One shouldn't start acting out of habit like meeting one's old chums. You should act after thinking about what you have to gain or lose. Some people don't go to *satsaṅgs* because they think they must swear off meat or alcohol. What greater madness is there than to let such fears deprive you of the company of the wise? When you yourself are not able to drop out of such habits, then you should cultivate a better quality of association. In good association lies the possibility of real gain. To remove the darkness, seek help from the light. In presence of light, darkness will end on its own. Your struggle should be to desire the light. Therefore, removing the mind from *saṃsāra*, you should turn it toward Paramātmā, and place your faith in Veda, *śāstra*, sādhus and *mahātmās*.

We say that we first serve *saṃsāra*, and after that, Bhagavān; then *saṃsāra* will not be obstructive. Serving *saṃsāra* is nothing but knowing its true form. In the beginning, the world itself becomes the guru. Whenever family members such as your own son insults you, then you become detached from the world.

Therefore, from the very beginning beware and practice keeping your mind directed on Bhagavān.

As long as we are capable of earning money, *samsārik* people love us. But you will not always be strong; one day old age will come, why shouldn't you understand this very day what family members are going to do with you in the future?

At this moment, we think they love us. When that stage comes, we will regret it. Then we will say, "My son is not listening to me, my daughter-in-law is not listening to me, those for whom I have done so much are now insulting me." This being the case, why should we do what will result in tears later? From this moment forward we should become careful. In *saṃsāra*, nobody belongs to anybody. Everyone stays together for their own benefit. As long as someone wants something, they will be affectionate towards you. So before you become disillusioned with these people, turn towards Bhagavān. If from this moment on you conduct Bhagavān's spiritual practice, then you won't be concerned about insults from your family members. The only one worthy of love is Paramātmā, so love him, and then you can be happy.

## *Teaching #92*

### To reach God, rely upon His name

ॐ

Hanumān was an unparalleled devotee of Bhagavān Rāma. He served Bhagavān endlessly. But he did not desire anything in return – this is endlessness. One does not have to instruct the highest order of servants; he just anticipates and spontaneously carries out the appropriate action. Bhagavān Rāma sent Hanumān to bring news about Sita, ordering him only to conduct reconnaissance. But Hanumān burned Lanka and challenged Rāvaṇa to a war, because he knew that Rāvaṇa had to be destroyed and that doing this would make Bhagavān happy. Bhagavān has said,

[Sanskrit:] *Durācārarato vāmi mannāmabhajanātka pe* ।

*Sālokyamuktamāpnoti na tu lokāntarādikam* ॥

This means, "Even the wicked person, if he worships me, will not go to the other world, but rather, he will gain *sālokya mokṣa*."[169]

---

[169] Viz., release within a world, the heaven which according to the *Bhakti* tradition is in close vicinity to the manifest god.

In *sālokya mokṣa*, there is still some delay before merging with Bhagavān, but one is freed fom taking birth again in any womb. Such people do not return to *saṃsāra*. When wicked people start worshipping Bhagavān, they become virtuous. This does not mean to go ahead and do bad things and evil in addition to worshiping Bhagavān. How can one who worships Bhagavān remain a wicked person?

To reach Bhagavān, rely upon His name. Bhagavān is ready to make you his own, but the failing is ours. Bhagavān takes care of the world with three hands, but keeps one hand empty. This is like women who bear water, stacking two pitchers on their head, holding a rope in one hand,[170] but keeping the other free. When the child starts crying to come into the mother's lap, then the mother says, "Catch hold of my leg so I can lift you with one hand. " None of her duties are interrupted. Creation, sustenance, and destruction—these are like the jars—engaged in these three activities, Bhagavān keeps one hand free for the sake of his devotees. But don't plan on being able to be lifted after grasping Bhagavān's feet. To serve and worship, to do his bhajan, are catching Bhagavān's feet. If you make Bhagavān your own, then He cannot stay far away from you. By worshipping Bhagavān, the body is cast off, and the poverty of many lives will be destroyed.

---

[170] Wells do not generally have ropes attached to them, so each person brings their own rope and pitchers to draw water.

# *Teaching #93*

**Sorrow has only apparent (*prātibhāsika*), not true (*vāstavika*) reality**

ॐ

Nowadays people everywhere seem peaceless and unhappy. The reason for this is the lack of real knowledge. This is clear to one who thinks with discrimination (*viveka*). External situations cannot influence us as long as we make a firm effort not to be influenced by them. Only when we let our minds believe so do external situations give happiness or sorrow. If we can continuously maintain the awareness that we are beyond the gross, subtle, and causal bodies, and that we are pure *sat chit ānanda ātman*, then no matter the situation, we cannot experience sorrow.

Experiencing our commenced (*prārabdha*) *karma* cannot be avoided. Both the enlightened and the ignorant have to experience it. The only difference is that the enlightened experience commenced *karma* pleasantly, be it good or bad, while the ignorant experiences all of it weeping. When it is certain that everyone has to experience commenced *karma*, then why not take it pleasantly? In reality there is no sorrow. It has but apparent existence (*prātibhāsika satta*), which can be seen as a mere by-product of delusion. It is like the case of seeing a rope in a dark room and imagining it to be a snake, due to which one experiences all the fears associated with the snake. Were you to see the rope in the light of the sun, you would neither worry, nor fear, nor tremble. Consider, perhaps, someone who happened to be among some people who imagine a snake in the rope and were afraid. In the same way, a knower may be in your midst, but sorrow cannot shake him.

If you discriminate, you will understand that the rope was the same for all. But the one who had seen it in the light will have no fear when he sees it in the darkness. Those who do not know its real nature due to delusion, thinking it to be a snake, will be afraid and sorrowful. If by some means the delusion were removed, then their sorrow will disappear as well. This clearly shows that the reason for the sorrow is delusion. Delusion can be removed, and therefore the sorrow can be removed. If sorrow were not born out of delusion, and if it had ultimate existence (*pāramārthika sattāvān*), then even the creator could not remove it, because something that is real (*sat*) can never be non-existent (*abhāva*).

Delusions can be destroyed in two ways, as illustrated by this same example of the snake and the rope. With the aid of a lamp, one can see the real form of the rope, and thereby the illusion of the snake can be removed. No one will be afraid of a rope. Only the illusion of a snake caused the problems of fear, trembling, etc. Hence because of the direct knowledge (*pratyakṣa jñāna*) of the underlying reality, its unreal aspects no longer remained. The second method of destroying delusion is to have firm faith in the words of the person who knows. By having faith in the words of he who has seen the rope in the daylight and who understands its nature correctly, fear can be removed.

Having completed spiritual practices such as discrimination (*viveka*), renunciation (*vairāgya*), six attainments (*sampatti*), and intense desire for liberation (*mumukṣutā*), through *samādhi* the knower can attain direct knowledge (*pratyakṣa jnāna*) of the world and *Brahman*'s true nature. He knows that Paramātmā pervades every form, whether *ātman* or non-*ātman*. Thus, although remaining in the world, [the knower] is beyond duality. By virtue of the knowledge gained in *samādhi*, he never feels any agony in daily affairs, because where ignorant people see danger, the knower sees Īśvara. For all the moving and unmoving, the single foundation of all the world is Paramātmā. When we come to see that the rope is the foundation of the snake, our fears dissipate. Similarly, when we understand that the foundation of the world is Paramātmā, then there will be no place for fear.

Even those who are incapable of direct knowledge of Paramātmā because of lack of spiritual practice, if they have faith and trust in the *śāstras*, and the works taught by a true guru established in *Brahman*, then their sorrow can be removed to a large extent. As long as there are misconceptions in the inner organ, even with the aid of thousands of devices, there will never be relief from sorrow. If you serve liquor to a distressed man and render him senseless, as long as he remains drunk, he forgets his pain. But when the effects of the alcohol wear off, he returns to his sorrowful state. Similarly, it isn't possible to get rid of sorrow by engaging the mind in worldly objects.

Knowing *ātman* will destroy all sorrow forever. This same consciousness is known by different names. Paramātmā pervades all living beings in the form of *ātman*. There is no difference between *ātman* and Paramātmā. That which is *ātman* is also known as *caitanya jīva*. The difference is only conditional (*upādhi*). Consciousness linked with condition (*upādhi*) is called *jīva*, and that consciousness which is free of all conditions is the *ātman*. The difference between *ātman* and *jīva* is like the difference between paddy and rice. As long as it is covered with a husk, it is called paddy, and when its husk is removed, it is called rice.

The practical difference between paddy and rice is that when paddy comes into contact with water and mud, it can sprout. But however long husked rice remains in contact with water and mud, it will not sprout into a plant. Similarly, as long as the bondage to good and bad action is present, the *caitanya jīva* will appear, and when the bondage due to actions is dissolved, there is awakened the pure *ātman*. Rebirth of *jīva* is like the sprouting. Good and bad *karma* is like the husk enclosing the *jīva*. By removing the outer husk, the grain cannot sprout. This means, if good and bad *karma* are renounced, then rebirth will not take place.

As long as the husk remains, we have only paddy. Even though the rice is inside, no one can boil and eat it. If somebody were to try to boil the paddy and eat it, he would be considered crazy. Similarly, as long as the bondage due to *karma* is not destroyed, the *jīva* will be deprived of the experience of supreme bliss.

Deluded by ignorance, the *jīva* falls into bondage to *karma*. Ignorance is called illusion (*bhrama*). It can only be removed by true knowledge. To attain knowledge, the help of the *śāstras* as well as a true guru (*Satguru*) are necessary. Knowledge of the *ātman* cannot be attained without the help of the guru, even if an individual struggles hard throughout his life. Recall the example of ten people, who were crossing a river, and they were all weeping, thinking that one person had drowned while crossing, until a *māhātma* came and removed their delusion. When the *māhātma* made them count again, and said "*daśavim tvam asi*," "you are the tenth," then their sorrow disappeared.[171] Similarly, only through the guru is it possible to become enlightened about "*Tat Tvam Asi*."[172]

Strengthen your faith in the existence of Bhagavān and his all-compassionate nature. Courageously face currently manifesting (*prārabdha)* *karma* and continue to do your enjoined activities as appropriate to your caste and stage of life. As you continue to practice your own *dharma*, your inner organ

---

[171] Ten people crossed the river, after which the leader said, "Let's count." The leader failed to count himself, so they started crying, thinking they were just nine, until a wise man pointed out that the leader was the tenth man: "You are the tenth."

[172] Guru Dev is making another pun. Playing off the phrase, "*daśavim tvam asi*," here he refers to the famous verse found in numerous *Upaniṣads*, "you are that," or *Tat tvam asi*, You (the *ātman*) are *Brahman*.

will be purified, and only then will you gain the worthiness to attain knowledge of *ātman*. You need not run away from your daily affairs for the sake of obtaining knowledge. Continue your daily affairs of the world (*saṃsāra*), but don't entangle your mind in them. *Saṃsāra* is not the cause for bondage, rather it is the attachment you have developed in the world (*saṃsāra*) which is the cause for bondage. Hence, renounce attachment and enjoy imperishable happiness. I am not speaking merely from book knowledge, I am speaking from my personal experience. If you follow these things with faith and fortitude then certainly you can become happy.

## *Teaching #94*

### ***Saṃsāra* is an ocean of sorrow; only the knower of the Self can cross it**

ॐ

When we look at *saṃsāra* with discernment, we see that there is not an iota of happiness there. To feel happy in this world is something like feeling pleasure while listening to your mother-in-law's insults. Abuse is abuse, how can it make you happy? Still, there are some people who have an attitude of desire toward the undesirable. It's like the drunkard who has fallen into a gutter and feels comfortable staying there. Even if someone tries to grab his hand and pull him out, he wants to stay put despite the effort. It is the same with those who feel happiness in *saṃsāra*. There is not an iota of happiness in its objects. *Saṃsāra* is only an ocean of sorrow. It is written, "*tarati śokam ātmavit*,"[173] the knower of

[173] Again, "the knower of *ātman* crosses sorrow.'' *Chāndogya Upaniṣad* Book 7, Chapter I, verse 3.

the self passes over the ignorance which is nothing but sorrow. *Śruti* says, "*ācāryavān puruṣo veda*," which means only he who has an *ācārya* knows puruṣa.[174] It does not say "the one with wealth knows *puruṣa*," or "the one with a son knows puruṣa" or "the one with a wife knows *puruṣa*," and so forth, nor one who has wife or a son.

Hence, in order to cross this ocean of sorrow, the ocean called *saṃsāra*, it is essential to obtain knowledge of the Self.

## *Teaching #95*

**Try to cross the vast ocean of becoming**

What greater misfortune is there than to drown while you are traveling in a boat?

ॐ

Every individual wants to be happy in this world and not spoil one's chances for the next. An atheist is someone who does not believe in the next world. Even the atheist wants to be happy and peaceful here. Believers want to make it in both worlds. But peace and happiness cannot be obtained merely by wishing. Desire propels one to act; peace and happiness can be obtained only with effort. Therefore when you try to obtain peace and happiness, your efforts should be legitimate (*vaidya*). By "legitimate" I mean that which is laid down in the *śāstras*. Some poet said,

[Sanskrit:] *na pītaṃ jāhnavī toyaṃ na gītaṃ bhagavad yaśaḥ* ।

[174] The term *puruṣa* means literally person, or man, but in its philosophical sense, it is the *ātman*, the abiding self.

*na jāne jānakī jāne jāne yamāhvāne kimuttaram* ||

I didn't drink the waters of the Ganges, now I have to see what will happen if I drink the waters of the Ganges? If by drinking the waters of the Ganges all my sins are destroyed, when sins are destroyed my intellect will be purified, and when my intellect is purified, love towards Bhagavān will increase. Such waters of the Ganges are available here. Such simplest of the simple means are available here.

Contemplating Bhagavān's love of devotees and singing are the praise of Bhagavān. To kill Hiraṇyakaśipu, Bhagavān manifested himself from a pillar, which is like using a cannon to kill an ant. For Bhagavān it was a very normal thing. Bhagavān could have changed Hiraṇyakaśipu's disposition had he wanted. But Prahalāda's nature was already decided; whenever he was thrown into something, he became the same element as that in which he was put. So when he was thrown into fire, he became fire. How can fire burn fire? When Prahalāda was dunked under water, he became water. But Bhagavān did all this in order to generate faith in his devotees, to keep them encouraged. To spread his glory he manifested himself directly in front of of Prahalāda. *Samsārik* people can say, "Why must Bhagavān act to spread his own glory?" But this was all due to his all encompassing love for his devotees, so that in the future, they would sing his praises about this glorious event, and cross the ocean of becoming. For this reason alone Bhagavān manifested himself to Prahalāda in the form of the Man-Lion.

During Draupadī's distress, Bhagavān became her sari itself. From remembering Bhagavān, contemplating and singing about him, the intellect will become purified and faith in Bhagavān will dawn. The means to know Bhagavān is to have faith in the Vedas and *śāstras*. If you do not have firm faith in the Vedas and *śāstras*, then you will not have firm faith in the very existence of

Bhagavān. If you do not have faith in the existence of Bhagavān, then doubt will remain. A doubting person cannot thrive in this or the next world.

If you do not know Bhagavān, and if you do not have faith in him, then where will you search for him? For example, if I have to go to a place called Ram Nagar, I will search for it on a map and will find it.Then I can stay in *Ātman Bhavan*.[175] The Veda and *śāstras* are the road map. With their help, you will find Bhagavān. However, just knowing Bhagavān is not sufficient, you must experience him. Experience is essential.

Solitude is a very good means for finding Bhagavān. Hence, remain in solitude and become an experienced *Māhātma*. Even people in *saṃsāra* can follow this — not just sannyasis — since even *Mahātmās* emerge from *saṃsāra* itself. *Mahātmās* don't come out of holes in the ground, but from some mother's womb. Today even those engrossed in bad and sinful activities can become one of the highest of *Mahātmās*.

Once I was chanting the *Upaniṣads*. A Paramahansa came and said, "What? You still worship and recite?" I was very surprised. I told him, "I am more surprised than you, because even though you are retired,[176] you are still bustling around offices. I am in a particular station of life, *sannyāsa*. You call yourself a Paramahansa, but a Paramahansa is supposed to be beyond all stations of life. Overseeing who is philandering in *saṃsāra* and who is carrying out worship is not your business. Your duty is supposed to be always staying in your

---

[175] *Ātman Bhavan*, literally building of the soul, was maintained by the King of Banaras as a resthouse for religious figures.

[176] The English word "retired" is in the original.

own self-nature. I am the principal; [177]I carry out worship and other things in order to teach others." The point is that the mind is so dishonest that one can cast off worship with the help of *Vedānta*, and not even realize that one has slipped. Good and bad actions always keep occurring according to currently manifesting (*prārabdha) karma*. Spiritual practice must necessarily continue for it to be carried out.

As long as currently manifesting (*prārabdha) karma* remains, one has to take up some work or another. Because of this, perform actions only after discriminating their propriety, and always while contemplating Bhagavān. The *śāstra* determines the propriety of an activity. This is not decided by some committee.[178] Our supervisor is the Vedas and *śāstras*. Continue to carry out your daily affairs. Keep your mind on Bhagavān. At the end, die while contemplating Bhagavān. If you cannot do this, you cannot do anything – despite being seated on a boat, you will have drowned in the river.

## *Teaching #96*

### There is no supporter other than Paramātmā

ॐ

Nobody will stay in *saṃsāra* forever. It is more like a lodging place. You have come here and obtained a rare human body, and are able to cross this ocean of becoming. Only with this [human] body can knowledge and devotion arise. If

---

[177] The English word "principal" is in the original.

[178] The English word "committee" is in the original.

you have not done it yet, then when will you do it? Paramātmā is all-pervasive everywhere; but we are present only in a particular location. Hence through *bhakti* we must make the all-pervading Paramātmā manifest itself in one particular location; only then will we succeed. What is the unmanifest and manifest? Fire is inherent within an entire piece of wood, but will not burn on its own. If you just put it in the hearth, and would like to make flatbread, can it cook? Once the wood is lit, and you make fire appear, then all your work will succeed.

Paramātmā is undivided in all space, time, and matter. There is no such thing anywhere in which Paramātmā is absent. Even though he is omnipotent, there is one power he doesn't have. Even if he wants, he cannot separate himself from us. Now you tell me, despite our being inseparable from Paramātmā, we are still unhappy, so whose side can be wrong?

Take the example of Draupadī. All her five husbands sat there, each more valorous than the last. Kripācharyā, Dronācharyā, and others just sat there, each greater charioteers than the last. A lady was dishonored. See the resignation of *samsārik* people; what greater shining example can one find than this? You can get some help from a father, son, brother, sister, or husband, but complete help is impossible from them. If Paramātmā doesn't come to our rescue in our times of trial, all our relatives will give up.

Except for Paramātmā, we have no support. It's absurd to feel that someone else will protect us. When great warriors gave up in resignation from helping Draupadī, what is the point of counting on your helpers? Maintain only polite relations with those in *saṃsāra*, don't become attached. Bhagavān came to rescue Draupadī only when she gave up hope in all the worldly people around her. In the case of Prahalāda, he manifested himself from a pillar. This shows the omnipresent nature of Bhagavān. But we don't benefit from the pervasive

Bhagavān. You cannot do your work with the fire inherent but unmanifest in wood. For work, wood has to be ignited so the fire is manifested in a particular place. Similarly, by making Paramātmā manifest himself by spiritual practice in a particular location, there can be benefit. For Bhagavān to manifest himself in a particular place is not difficult because he himself declared,

[Sanskrit:] *yadā yadā hi dharmasya glānir bhavati bhārata* ।

*abhyuthānam adharmasya tadātmānaṁ sṛjāmyaham* ॥

*paritrāṇāya sādhūnāṁ vināśāya ca duṣkṛtām* ।

*dharmasaṁsthāpanārthāya sambhavāmi yuge yuge* ॥[179]

Not only this, but he has also said,

[Sanskrit:] *ye yathā māṁ prapdyante tāṁstathaiva bhajāmyaham* ।[180]

This means, "However one remembers me, so do I remember him." What a great assurance Bhagavān has given. If we do not want him even now, then alas, it is our great misfortune.

---

[179] *Bhagavad Gītā* 4.7-4.8.

[180] *Bhagavad Gītā* 4.11ab.

# *Teaching #97*

**Caste ranking is not beneficial**

ॐ

One's birth is determined by one's *karma*, but Bhagavān's compassion is not determined by *karma* but rather by a person's disposition. Anyone — whether Brahmin, Kṣatriya, Vaiśya, or Śūdra — can obtain Bhagavān if he strives for him with intense feeling. Only a human being can praise Bhagavān, it isn't the case that only Brahmins can praise him. A *bhakta* can belong to any of the four *varṇas*, but an *ācharyā* cannot be a person from just any of the four *varṇas*. Śri Ādi Śāṅkarācharyā proclamated about this,

[Sanskrit:] *yāvadvittopārjanasaktastāvannijaparivāro raktaḥ* ।

*paścājjīvati jarjara dehe vārtāṁ ko'pi na pṛcchati gehe* ॥ [181]

For this reason, worship Govinda, worship Govinda, worship Govinda, O foolish one.

Whoever one may be, to whatever caste one may belong, one should become extremely cautious that before becoming too old, do sufficient worship of Bhagavān. Only this will lead to ultimate good. Wellbeing is not assured by mere birth in a particular caste. Wellbeing is possible only through the worship of Bhagavān, which can only be done by a human being. It is untrue that only a

---

[181] This is *Bhaja Govinda* verse 5-6. The *Bhaja Govinda* is attributed to Śri Ādi Śāṅkarācharyā. For an excellent introduction to the hymns purportedly created by him, see T. M. P. Mahadevan's *The Hymns of Śaṅkara* (Delhi: Motilal Banarsidass, reprint 1986). I quote Mahadevan's translation on page 46: "As long as you have the ability to earn money, so long will your dependents be attached to you. After that, when you live with an infirm body, no one would even speak to you a word."

Brahmin can become liberated. If a person has devotion towards Bhagavān, that is well and good. Otherwise even a Brahmin can be eligible to go to hell. And a devoted Śūdra can attain Bhagavān. In terms of wellbeing, there is no Brahmin, no Kṣatriya, no Vaiśya, and no Śūdra. In the ultimate goal, there are no differences: differences only exist in daily affairs.

## *Teaching #98*

**To become wicked toward the wicked and to abuse those who abuse us is not correct**

[Sanskrit:] *kṣamā khaḍgaḥ kare yasya durjanaḥ kim kariṣyati* ।

This means, "One who is holding the sword of forgiveness cannot be troubled by the wicked."

[Sanskrit:] *atṛne patite trahiḥ svayam evopaśamyati* ॥

Where there is no piece of straw, what can a spark do? It will die out on its own. Similarly, wickedness done to a forgiving person will stop on its own. For this reason, one should always take the attitude of equanimity (*upekṣa*).

ॐ

One should carry out all one's actions by staying in one of these four attitudes: friendliness, compassion, cheerfulness, and equanimity.[182] One should not rely on any other attitude. If you follow this advice, you will not experience occasions of peacelessness.

---

[182] These four qualities are also the four cardinal virtues of yoga, classical Buddhism, and much of popular Hinduism.

There are few points regarding the misuse of wealth. The number one[183] misuse for wealth is spending it on wicked activities. The number two misuse is not to apply one's earnings toward preparing for the future. Even if wealth is not spent on bad activities, if it is not used for good activities, then it is still a misuse. Thus the number two misuse occurs if the money is not spent on bad activities, but at the same time, it is not spent on good works, either.

The proper use of wealth is the first way, meaning spending it only on worthy activities.

One should always endeavor to make proper use of this life. Nowadays people waste their most precious time in unnecessary arguments of caste and sect. Taking birth in one caste or another is a fact of life, but turning their backs on Bhagavān they are entangling themselves in forming groups of castes. Wherever one might have taken birth, he should try his best to come out of the prison of birth and death. One should not continue to support another prison called caste. One should profit from caste and sect to this extent — one should adopt whatever good may be recommended in the Vedas and *śāstras*, and stay away from and abandon whatever things that are prohibited according to Vedas and *śāstras*. This way, caste pride is meaningful. Have certainty that a good thing is only that which is in accordance with the Veda and *śāstra*. Nothing will become good or bad according to our thinking. That is good which the Vedas and *śāstras* declare to be good, and that is bad which the Vedas and *śāstras* declare to be bad.

---

[183] Guru Dev uses the English expressions "number one" and "number two" in the original.

If you are desire wealth, then collect that wealth which can accompany you [after death]. What is the use of accumulating wealth which is temporary[184] and has to be left behind in this world?

One thing is certain; because of lack of discrimination, *dhanāśā jīvitāśā ca jiryato 'pinajīryate* |. The desire to acquire wealth and stay alive will not depart even those on their death bed. Here's an illustration.

Once there lived a very old lady. Somehow she survived by selling pieces of firewood picked up from here and there. Her life was full of misery. One day while picking up firewood from the forest, she became greedy and picked up so much wood that her bundle was too heavy to lift onto her head, even though she tried time after time to lift it. In the end, she gave up all hope. Out of disgust she said, "If death were to come somehow, then I would be free from misery." She had barely uttered these words when Death appeared in front of her. Death asked, "Tell me, dear mother, why have you called me?" The old lady asked, "Who are you?" Death said, "I am Death; you called me, so I came." The old lady said, "Very good, you have come, I called you to carry this bundle."

The point is, no matter what state a person may be in, if he's still breathing, he does not want to die. But if one is living just by eating and drinking, such a life is of no use. Life will be meaningful only if it is lived is such a way that it prepares for the future. If life is devoted only to the enjoyment of sense pleasures, and thus to acquiring sin, then it is better to die than to live.

You should always try to remember while carrying out daily affairs to make sure that even if your activities cannot be of benefit anyone, then at least

---

[184] The English word "temporary" is in the original.

they should do no harm.[185] Along with this you should carry out at least some amount of worship and contemplation of Bhagavān. The mind is always fickle. But whether the mind is concentrated or not, one should spend some time in worship and prayer. If your mind is not focused now, it will become more sharply focused after a few days, but you must keep doing it. If you drink water from the same glass, after a few days, you will become fond of that glass, and if you are offered water in another glass, you tend to inquire, "where is that old glass?" Similarly, you will come to love the walking cane that you constantly hold in your hand after just a few days. In the same fashion, as you continue to chant the name of Bhagavān, you will start loving it like that glass and walking cane. For this reason, even if you are not able to keep your mind concentrated, you should continue to chant the name of Bhagavān. Let the mind go anywhere.

## *Teaching #99*

**Freed from both giving up and acquiring, dissolve into the bliss of your essential nature**

What do you give up?

ॐ

From the very beginning the world (*saṃsāra*) is already given up. Sound, form, taste, smell, etc., whatever other materials are there, are already different from you. Their existence is different from you. When the world (*saṃsāra*) is

---

[185] This is a humorous pun. Guru Dev here contrasts *bhalāī*—benefit/goodness—with *burāī*—harm/evil.

different from you anyway, then what can you give up? Even before you can give them up, they are already given up, because they are different from you. Because of this, thinking or talking about giving things up is false, a kind of empty boasting. What is the glory in slaying the slain? Will anyone shoot a dead tiger and say, "I have hunted a lion"? This is like someone saying, "I have given up such and such thing." In this world (*saṃsāra*) everything is already given up. Nothing can be designated as a thing fit to be given up. All things, by their own nature, you have already given up.

What can you acquire?

There is nothing fit to be acquired in this world. What can you acquire? Whatever things you may see, all are unreal, like the magician's money. There is no real substance in them. A thing can be called fit to be acquired if it gives peace and happiness. All objects of the world (*saṃsāra*) are transient, and all will end in separation. The sorrow which we get when we are separated from them will be much greater than the happiness which we get while acquiring them, and even the change we undergo in acquiring them give sorrow. Thus the union will ultimately end in sorrow. That is why no object here is worth acquiring; in the world (*saṃsāra*), there is nothing at all worth acquiring.

If you look towards the essential nature, then you can see with the sentiment, *sarvam khalvidam brahma*—this whole world is *Brahman.*[186] There is nothing other than this essential nature. Thus, if everything is the same as your essential nature, and there is nothing different from this, then what can really be acquired? In this fashion also, there is nothing to gain in this world (*saṃsāra*).

---

[186] *Chāndogya Upaniṣad* 3.14.1.

Thus, however you look at it, there is nothing fit to be gained in this world (*saṃsāra*).

That is why it is said you should not desire to acquire or give up anything. Stay completely away from giving up and acquiring. When you have no desire to acquire or give up anything, then you will be free from your past tendencies (*vāsanā*) and will become established in your essential nature (*svarūpa*). Thus, contemplate and firmly understand in your mind that there is nothing to be given up or gained. After establishing this thought, immerse yourself in the bliss of your essential nature. Therein lies the fulfillment of human birth.

## *Teaching #100*

**Lack of discrimination causes humans endless difficulties**

ॐ

The all-blissful, omnipotent Bhagavān dwells within all. He is in the hearts of everyone, inseparable from all. Even so, people seem to be unhappy and unpeaceful. Yet all of the unhappiness and turbulence in the world is due to only one thing — lack of discrimination. The treasure house of peace and happiness, Bhagavān, resides within, but because of lack of discriminative thinking, people search outside here and there for peace and happiness. They think that acquiring various physical things will lead to happiness, when this is actually the root cause of all unhappiness.

What more can be said when Draupadī herself was deluded? When Dhūśāasana leapt up and began trying to disrobe her, she turned to each one of her great warrior husbands, and also to the great father Bhiṣma. When nobody could stir from their seats to help, then Draupadī understood that in her time of trial, no one could be of real assistance. Even the greatest physical strength will be useless at such a time, and all one's supporters will turn their faces away. Realizing her helpless situation, she remembered Bhagavān Kṛṣṇa and she called out to him, "O Protector, O Dweller in Dwaraka!"

Now, think about this: If Draupadī had been using right discrimination, she would not have addressed Bhagavān as the one who dwells in Dwaraka. Bhagavān is the ever-present within one's own heart. Instead of seeing Bhagavān within herself, she called him from Dwaraka; this is lack of discrimination. Not to consider the omnipotent Bhagavān as the ever Omnipresent everywhere is the greatest of non-discrimination. Just because of this, people suffer greatly and fail to receive the grace of Bhagavān.

Only when Draupadī's sari started growing did she understand that Bhagavān had come. Then she said, "Bhagavān, you delayed a bit in coming." Bhagavān replied, " Draupadī, I was in fact very close to you, but you called me from Dwaraka. So first I had to go there and then come back, which was the reason for the delay."

It is clear that Bhagavān is omnipresent in all and is always ready to shower his grace on his devotees.

"Whoever worships me in whatever way, so do I accept it." This is the pledge of Bhagavān:

[Sanskrit:] *ye yathā māṁ prapdyante tāṁstathaiva bhajāmyaham* |[187]

---

[187] *Bhagavad Gītā* 4.11ab.

Hence, believing in the all-pervading nature of Bhagavān, carry out your spiritual practice and become a fit vessel for his grace. Then you will be free from unhappiness and peacelessness once and for all.

## *Teaching #101*

### Selfishness is very powerful

ॐ

Selfishness is so predominant in the world (*saṃsāra*) that if some day human skin becomes useful for some reason, it will be removed and only then will a corpse be sent to the funeral pyre [crematorium]. There is no doubt about this. As long as one fulfills people's selfishness, they will all respond with respect and love. Bhagavān Ādi Śāṅkarācharyā rightly said:

[Sanskrit:] *yāvadvittopārjanasaktastāvannijaparivāro raktaḥ* ।
*paścājjīvati jarjara dehe vārtāṁ ko'pi na pṛcchati gehe* ॥[188]

This means, as long as one has the capacity to earn, one's family members show love. But when old age comes, and the body is totally spent, then nobody in the house will even inquire about him.[189] Therefore, "Worship Govinda, worship Govinda. O foolish thinking one, worship Govinda." Hey ignorant one! Foolish soul! Worship Bhagavān![190]

---

[188] This is *Bhaja Govinda* verse 5-6.

## *Teaching #102*

### Materialism cannot give peace and happiness

ॐ

All material prosperity is nothing but the unfolding of *māyā*. Trying to obtain peace and happiness through engagement with *māyā* is like trying to search darkness with darkness. Just as you can't kill a snake by taking a stick and pounding on the ground above its lair, you cannot remove the peacelessness of the subtle body by acquiring objects for physical pleasure. Happiness and unhappiness reside in the mind. If you insult a sleeping person, he will not feel unhappy, because at that time his mind is absorbed in ignorance. This means that the mind alone experiences happiness or unhappiness. Because of this, as long as the mind is unsatiated, lack of peace cannot be dispelled. As long as the mind wanders, it cannot obtain the all-blissful Bhagavān. Just as you give toys to little children to divert them, you can divert your mind with wealth, a wife, children, name and fame, etc. But these things cannot satisfy the mind. The mind will only be satisfied once it obtains the biggest possible thing. In *saṃsāra*, Paramātmā alone is the greatest of all things. After knowing it, nothing else is worthy to be known.

## *Teaching #103*

### Have faith in fate for your livelihood

Do not acquire sin by carrying out wrong actions due to pressures from someone.

ॐ

[Sanskrit:] *yadasmadīyaṃ na hi tatpareśām* ।

We are certain to get whatever is our fate, no one else can get it. This is an infallible law according to the *Karma Mīmāmsa Śāstra*. I have experienced this many times myself. It's like a thick uninhabitable forest, where no human can even be imagined to dwell. Your fate will follow you even there. Currently manifesting (*prārabdha) karma*'s effects will also follow there. When currently manifesting (*prārabdha) karma* is over, then the body will be cast off. One thing is certain, that as long as one is embodied, currently manifesting (*prārabdha) karma* must be experienced. There is no doubt about this. Because of this, to be worried about one's own ability and welfare, indicates one's forgetfulness about his past accumulations.

Whatever has been earned in the past, will without doubt be experienced. However much money has been deposited in the bank, the same can be withdrawn. What is to doubt about it? Now money in a bank in *saṃsāra*—sometimes a bank can fail, and go under—but the results of whatever actions you perform will be deposited in a bank that can never fail. That is the inexhaustible treasury of the omniscient, omnipotent one, in whose accounts there cannot be any mistake. Therefore, however one has acted, so must one experience its results, bit by bit.

Whatever comes near you is your currently manifesting (*prārabdha) karma* to be experienced. But whatever comes along should be experienced with discrimination. The only difference between a human being and an animal is that the animal cannot discriminate propriety, what is proper and improper. As you are all human beings, conduct your daily affairs discriminating between proper and improper action.

Never carry out any kind of action due to someone's pressure or shyness that will result in your accumulating sin. The path ahead will be spoiled because of sin. Whatever you have carried out earlier, you are enjoying the fruits of the same. Taking a lesson from this, improve your future by carrying out superior actions now. Don't start supporting all good and bad actions of a person just because he gives you food and clothing; *jākara khāī tākava duhāī.*[191] Dogs act like that. A human being should act only with discrimination. Support only proper actions, and if you cannot oppose improper actions, at least remain neutral.

## *Teaching #104*

### Carry out good actions as much as possible

The bliss born out of the realization of *ātman* is possible only through the control of the senses, not through the enjoyment of sense objects

ॐ

The senses experience sound, touch, sight, taste, and smell. Since the senses are all extroverted, they can obtain knowledge only related to external things. The senses cannot gain the knowledge of internal matters. *Ātman* is that which is closest to us. It is always available. It is never absent from our experience. Nevertheless, we are not able to see it, nor are we able to know it.

[191] "You go off to eat, you go off to bark."

How can we see the One who sees everything? The eyes see everything but they cannot see themselves. To see them, a mirror is required. The mirror to see *ātman* is the inner organ (*antaḥ karaṇa*). *Antaḥ* means inner, and *karaṇa* means the tool to obtain knowledge. Because it is the means to inner knowledge, it is called *"antaḥ karaṇa."* Only if the mirror is clean will the reflection be clear. If the mirror is unclean, the reflection will be obscured. Similarly, a pure *antaḥ karaṇa* reflects *ātman*; people whose inner organ is impure cannot see it. Therefore it is essential to purify the *antaḥ karaṇa*.

It is ignorant to be proud of one's caste, sect, beauty, youth, wealth, reputation, etc. As long as one doesn't cast off such vanities, how is knowledge of the soul possible? Only when ignorance is destroyed will knowledge about the Self be gained. An ignorant person thinks that he is different from Paramātmā, and that the gross body is his true self. He becomes attached to the perishable things of this world. Because of this he grasps at one thing or another, and remains unhappy.

The *śāstras* and gurus say that this world is illusory (*mithyā*). The "illusory" is that which can be seen, but has no permanent existence. It's like the case of mistakenly taking a rope to be a snake in dim light, when the existence of the snake is not real. Despite the state of error, the appearance is true. Until one discovers the reality of the rope, even if a person conducts an *aśvamedha* sacrifice[192] and spends tens of thousands of rupees to get rid of it, this illusion will still remain. The only method to remove it is by bringing a lamp, and seeing

---

[192] An elaborate sacrifice with royal origins featuring the sacrifice of a horse (*aśva*), ordinarily sponsored only by the rich and powerful for great desires.

the actual form of the rope in its light. Once the knowledge of the rope is awakened, the individual will no longer be able to see it as a snake, even if he tries. Similarly, he who has awakened to the knowledge of Paramātmā will not be able to see this world as real. Only an ignorant person takes it to be real. The unreality of this world can be understood only if one wakes up from the sleep of ignorance. In order to wake up from this state, one need not go to the forest. One cannot obtain knowledge merely by living in a forest. I do not know how many Kol and Bhil tribal peoples[193] there are living in the forest, but they are great fools. Solitude is useful when it is employed in spiritual practice intent on removing this ignorance. The spiritual practices to remove ignorance should be obtained from a *satguru* and the *śāstras*. But how can this ignorance be removed if one does not have sufficient faith in the *śāstras*, and in the words of *mahātmās*? Thus, it is necessary to cultivate faith.

[Sanskrit:] *asaṁśayavatāṁ muktiḥ saṁśayāviṣṭa cetasām* |
*na muktirjanma janmānte tasmād viśvāsamāpnuyāt* ||

In summary, the meaning of liberation is to not return to this world (*saṃsāra*). The second meaning is that one is not touched by sorrows.

He who doesn't have the latent tendencies and attachments towards wife, children, wealth, respect, fame, etc., can definitely experience *ātman*. Only one

---

[193] The Kols and Bhils are groups who live in the vast range of forests in the Vindhya mountains, a range which bifurcates north and south India. Guru Dev spoke elsewhere of wandering in the Vindhya regions, so here he may be speaking from his own experience and assessments of the forest dwellers' nature.

who has understood *ātman* in its essential form will be able to cross this ocean of sorrow.

The inner organ is sullied by latent tendencies, therefore it is essential to destroy these tendencies. One should not try to satiate latent tendencies (*vāsanās)* by enjoying sensory objects because *na bhūto na bhavīṣyati* —it's never happened, and it never can happen. Satiation is possible only through discrimination, whether you accomplish that today or after ten years. The senses can be pacified only through discrimination. Through enjoyment the latent impressions to enjoy will only be strengthened. If itching could be cured by scratching, then we might have hope to satisfy the senses through enjoyment of objects.

Everyone knows that nothing comes along with us after death. Our own body goes only so far as the funeral pyre. But have faith in the Vedas and *śāstras*, and then one thing will follow you. Only the good and bad actions of this life follow a person to the next world. Those who have done good actions attain superior worlds, and those who have done bad actions go to hell. Therefore, as much as possible, carry out good actions.

# *Teaching #105*

**Be alert and utilize this life properly**

ॐ

There are three things in this world (*saṃsāra*): body, mind, and wealth.[194] When body, mind, and wealth are properly employed, then there is no prospect for lack of peace. If they are not properly employed, one experiences peacelessness. However, there is no school or college to teach their proper use.[195]

Wealth ends in three ways. That which is not given in charity, or used for one's own enjoyment, ends up in the third way, which is its dissipation. Tulasīdās has written, "*so dhana dhanya, pratham gati jākī.*"

This means that wealth which is spent in the first way [charity] is useful. Tulasīdās Ji spoke only of wealth, but I say,

[Hindi:] *so dhana dhanya, pratham gati jākī, so mana dhanya, pratham gati jākī.*

This means that body and mind are useful which end up in the first way.

The best use of the body is to engage it in worship of Bhagavān. The eyes should see the form of Bhagavān, the ears should hear about his glories, speech should praise him—every one of the sense organs should engage in matters related to Bhagavān alone. Even one's breath should be engaged exclusively in the worship of Bhagavān. The first end of the mind also must be to

---

[194] This is a poetic triad: *tana*, *mana*, and *dhana*.

[195] The English words "school" and "college" are in the original.

continuously engage itself in Bhagavān. The first end of wealth has already been said, wealth should be given in charity, but even before considering charity, propriety should be considered to make sure that this wealth has been earned through right means. It's wrong to earn money regardless of how it can be attained. Whatever wealth is earned through unworthy and sinful actions, will remain here, but the result of the sins will go with you and will not leave. That is why one should not commit sins while earning wealth. The sins will not remain behind with the money. Hence one should think carefully while earning wealth.

One *Māhātma* had obtained a *siddhi* by which he was able to tell both the good and bad actions of any person who approached him. Once I happened to meet him. While wandering around, I happened to show up in his location.[196] I said to him, "The world goes on sinning, and you are worried about it. This is a great loss. Rather than contemplating Paramātmā, to worry about undesireable and evil deeds is a misuse of the mind. And after becoming a sādhu, that there should be such misuse of the mind!!"

Another great misuse of body and mind is for people to begin supporting castes and sects. You have obtained the body of a human being; you've been born into some caste or another, be it Brahmin, Kṣatriya, Vaiśya, or Śūdra. In whatever *varṇa* you have been born within, everyone is authorized to remember Bhagavān, and everyone is eligible to become close to Bhagavān.There will be some class[197] differences, but this is not something which should be over-

---

[196] Guru Dev reveals here that he did not seek this fellow out.

[197] The English word "class" is in the original.

emphasized. Wherever your birth has taken place, it's over now. Now you should try to live in such a way that you will not take birth again. You should not waste your precious time in supporting the caste in which you have taken birth.This world is like a way station. After coming here you should work for the main goal, not to support this way station. In human life, it is improper for the mind, which is supposed to be engaged in Bhagavān, to be engaged in wrong or trivial activities.

## *Teaching #106*

### Only by focusing with discrimination is the mind directed to the good path

ॐ

The leader of this indivisible universe, the all-blissful, *sat chit ānanda*, Bhagavān, has been revealed in the Vedas. By taking up the path of the Vedas, one can know Him. The Veda is not manmade, it bestows divine sight. To see the divine true form of Bhagavān, divine sight is required. The vision of Bhagavān's true form cannot be obtained with this gross physical eye; as Bhagavān taught Arjuna in the *[Bhagavad] Gita*

[Sanskrit:] *Na tu māṃ śakyase draṣṭum anenaiva svacakṣuṣā* I *divyaṃ dadāmi te cakṣuḥ paśya me yogam aiśvaram.* (*Bhagavad Gītā* 11.8)

To wish to obtain divine sight is the ultimate goal. Human life is fulfilled through this.

Only elemental things (the gross physical) can be seen with the physical eye. In fact, for different things, there are different types of vision. Not all things can be seen in the same way of seeing. Consider, for example: mother and father, brother and sister, wife, etc., all have similar physical bodies. Is it possible to see all of them with the same vision? A mother is seen with one vision, whereas one's sister and of course one's wife are seen another way. Furthermore, the same object is seen differently by different people, according to their station and level of attainment (*adhikāra*).

Similarly, spiritual practice also differs according to the differences in each person's station and level of attainment. The root of all Vedas is *praṇava* (om]. But not all have the eligibility to chant this *mantra*. *Praṇava* is pure *Brahman*. Only a Sannyāsi who has given up all attachment to physical things and who is thus a *samyakanyāsī*, for him alone there will be no attachment or hatred for the things of this world (*saṃsāra)* is eligible. He stays alone, aloof, one apart from everything. Only such a person is eligible to chant the pure *praṇava*. A householder who has attachment towards his household, wife, and children, is not eligible to chant the *praṇava*. This is because the intended results of chanting the *praṇava* are to become the purified Brahman, devoid of *māyā*, whose true form is solitary *sat, chit, ananda*. The *japa* of *praṇava* will not yield good results for a householder, and instead will lead to destructive and inauspicious results. That is why it has been enjoined that householders should not utter the *praṇava* by itself, but rather, they should join some *mantra* with *praṇava* and chant them together. Hence, *praṇava* should be prefixed to a *mantra* and then chanted. Not doing it like this is unauthorized. Unauthorized practice will have no power to transform the heart, and all one's efforts will go to waste.

Generally people say that their restlessness of mind is not diminishing and that their mind is not settling down. But restlessness in the mind can be calmed only by carrying out one's various daily and enjoined duties. If they don't do this, and then they imagine that by sitting in meditation, they will immediately attain it—how can this be successful?

The mind flows towards sound, touch, sight, taste and smell, and it becomes impure through continued contact with sense objects. How can it move toward purity? The mind's movement is like that of a dog. Desiring happiness, it runs here and there, sometimes pursuing some sight, sometimes some smell, sometimes some touch, sometimes some sound; the dog-like mind runs around, and cannot settle down. When one is always enjoying sensory objects, how can one enjoy *ātman*? If one leaves objects and turns towards *ātman*, then only will one become an enjoyer of *ātman* rather than sensory objects. He whose mind is bent toward Bhagavān will not run off to see the cinema. He who starts loving the beauty of Bhagavān will not even bat an eye at any object of the world (*saṃsāra*). One who starts enjoying the imperishable happiness in touching the feet of Bhagavān will not desire the touch of physical things.

So turn this mind, running like a dog after beauty, taste, smell, touch, and sound, in the direction of some manifest form of Bhagavān. Pour your nature into experiencing the pleasurable touch of its service. Learn to offer incense to Bhagavān, and accept all offerings as his grace (*prasād*).

## *Teaching #107*

### Whoever has forgotten his goal will miss his path

ॐ

The ultimate goal of human life is to obtain the all-blissful, omnipotent, very essence of knowledge: Paramātmā. One who always remembers the supreme goal and always follows the path laid down by the Vedas and *śāstras* in order to achieve it—meaning one who engages his whole being, his body, senses, mind, intellect, etc., according to the path laid down in the *śāstras*, and thus strictly leads his life according to *dharma*—he alone in reality is using his free will properly, and he alone is really fortunate. Only such a person will be able to fulfill all his desires, and he will definitely reach his ultimate goal, without any doubt.

The ones who make this their ultimate goal seek the help of an expert in this subject. Endowed with faith, make one such person your guide so that you can benefit from all his experience. Another point is that all your life's activities should be in harmony with the achievement of your ultimate goal and should not become a hindrance.

Every moment of your life you should be alert, lest you stray from your path to attain the ultimate goal. Do not forget that the daily affairs will lead to the ultimate. If your daily affairs are in accord with your eligibility as dictated by the *śāstras*, then it will hasten your progress to gaining your goal. If your mind becomes entrapped in sense experience and becomes a slave to its desires, then your daily affairs will not be in accordance with the limits set by the *śāstra*. Then your daily affairs will remove you from the right path and will take you away from your ultimate goal.

Consequently, it is necessary to always remember your ultimate goal, follow the guidance of an experienced guru, and ever alert, act in accordance with the path of humility directed to the guru's feet to attain your goal.

## *Teaching #108*

### There is no lack of anything for the one who has turned towards Bhagavān

ॐ

By doing *satsaṅga*, discrimination arises, awakening one to what is proper and improper, merit and sin, *adharma* and duty. That is why one who does *satsaṅga* is saved from *adharma* and engages himself in *dharma*. Saved from sin, he will carry out meritorious activities. Established doctrines (*siddhānta*), *dharmeṇa pāpamanuda[n]ti*, [198] that by practicing *dharma*, sin is destroyed. Similarly, *satsaṅga* also destroys sin.

By listening to discussions about Bhagavān, sitting in *satsaṅga,* the internal sorrow and anxiety which naturally scorch the human heart are cleansed and pacified, and the inner organ will naturally become peaceful.

Through *satsaṅga* the human being turns towards the omnipotent, all-capable Bhagavān. One who is ever turned towards Bhagavān will have no lack

---

[198]*Mahānarāyaṇa Upaniṣad*, Chapter 22 verse 1.

of anything in the world. All his sorrow and misery will be destroyed. In this way, by association with saints, all sins, misery, and poverty will be totally eliminated.

May there always be auspiciousness *(śubham astu nityam)*.

CPSIA information can be obtained
at www.ICGtesting.com
Printed in the USA
LVHW031611150719
624133LV00004B/473/P

9 781304 662002